IT'S IN THE BAG!

Tasty Gifts in Crafty Sacks

*S*ay good-bye to overpriced gift bags, wrong-size boxes, and ho-hum wrappings for your gifts from the kitchen! When you're searching for the perfect present — and the perfect presentation — look no further than the pages of this exciting new volume. It's in the Bag! *is brimming with ideas for sprucing up inexpensive bags to coordinate with your food gifts: brown bags, white lunch sacks, large grocery bags, tiny penny sacks, plain gift bags, and so many more. Why cover those beautiful cookies with aluminum foil when you can use our simple craft techniques and easy instructions to present them in extraordinary gift bags, all at a fraction of gift shop prices! Making creative surprises has never been easier, and just wait till you see how much fun it can be. For any reason and every season, we have the answer to all your gift-giving needs — and* It's in the Bag!

Anne Childs

LEISURE ARTS, INC.
Little Rock, Arkansas

IT'S IN THE BAG!

Tasty Gifts in Crafty Sacks

EDITORIAL STAFF

Vice President and Editor-in-Chief: Anne Van Wagner Childs
Executive Director: Sandra Graham Case
Editorial Director: Susan Frantz Wiles
Publications Director: Carla Bentley
Creative Art Director: Gloria Bearden
Senior Graphics Art Director: Melinda Stout

DESIGN
Design Director: Patricia Wallenfang Sowers
Designers: Katherine Prince Horton, Sandra Spotts Ritchie, Linda Diehl Tiano, Rebecca Sunwall Werle, and Anne Pulliam Stocks
Executive Assistant: Billie Steward

FOODS
Foods Editor: Celia Fahr Harkey, R.D.
Assistant Foods Editor: Jane Kenner Prather
Test Kitchen Home Economist: Rose Glass Klein
Test Kitchen Coordinator: Nora Faye Taylor
Test Kitchen Assistants: Leslie Belote Dunn and Susan Scott

ART
Book/Magazine Graphics Art Director: Diane M. Hugo
Senior Production Graphics Artist: Michael A. Spigner
Photography Stylist: Christina Tiano Myers

TECHNICAL
Managing Editor: Kathy Rose Bradley
Technical Editor: Leslie Schick Gorrell
Technical Writers: Carol A. Reed, Margaret F. Cox, and Briget Julia Laskowski
Technical Associate: Kimberly J. Smith

EDITORIAL
Managing Editor: Linda L. Trimble
Associate Editors: Tammi Williamson Bradley and Andrea Isaac Adams
Assistant Editors: Terri Leming Davidson, Robyn Sheffield-Edwards, and Darla Burdette Kelsay
Copy Editor: Laura Lee Weland

PROMOTIONS
Managing Editors: Tena Kelley Vaughn and Marjorie Ann Lacy
Associate Editors: Steven M. Cooper, Dixie L. Morris, and Jennifer Leigh Ertl
Designer: Rhonda H. Hestir
Art Director: Linda Lovette Smart
Production Artist: Leslie Loring Krebs
Publishing Systems Administrator: Cindy Lumpkin
Publishing Systems Assistant: Susan Mary Gray

BUSINESS STAFF

Publisher: Bruce Akin
Vice President, Marketing: Guy A. Crossley
Marketing Manager: Byron L. Taylor
Print Production Manager: Laura Lockhart
Vice President and General Manager: Thomas L. Carlisle
Retail Sales Director: Richard Tignor

Vice President, Retail Marketing: Pam Stebbins
Retail Marketing Director: Margaret Sweetin
Retail Customer Services Manager: Carolyn Pruss
General Merchandise Manager: Russ Barnett
Vice President, Finance: Tom Siebenmorgen
Distribution Director: Ed M. Strackbein

Table of Contents

Table of Contents

Table of Contents

CANDIED CORN CONFETTI

For festive New Year's favors, dress up plain sacks with glitter paint and a rainbow of ribbon and star garland. Fill them with Jelly Bean Candied Corn for gifts that will dazzle!

JELLY BEAN CANDIED CORN

  8 quarts popped white popcorn
12 ounces small gourmet jelly beans
  3 cups sugar
1$^{1}/_{2}$ cups light corn syrup
$^{3}/_{4}$ cup butter or margarine
$^{1}/_{2}$ cup water
$^{1}/_{2}$ teaspoon salt
$^{1}/_{2}$ teaspoon baking soda
$^{1}/_{2}$ teaspoon raspberry-flavored oil
$^{1}/_{8}$ teaspoon red liquid food coloring

Combine popcorn and jelly beans in a greased large roasting pan; set aside. Butter sides of a 4$^{1}/_{2}$-quart Dutch oven. Combine sugar, corn syrup, butter, water, and salt in Dutch oven. Stirring constantly, cook over medium-low heat until sugar dissolves. Using a pastry brush dipped in hot water, wash down any sugar crystals on sides of pan. Attach a candy thermometer to pan, making sure thermometer does not touch bottom of pan. Increase heat to medium-high and bring to a boil. Cook, without stirring, until mixture reaches soft-crack stage (approximately 280 to 290 degrees). Test about $^{1}/_{2}$ teaspoon mixture in ice water. Mixture will form hard threads in ice water but will soften when removed from the water. Remove from heat and stir in baking soda, raspberry oil, and food coloring. Pour over popcorn mixture; stir

until well coated. Spread popcorn mixture on greased aluminum foil to cool. Break into pieces. Store in an airtight container.

Yield: about 36 cups candied corn (6 gifts)

"HAPPY NEW YEAR!" BAG

For each bag, you will need a white lunch bag, a 12" square of clear cellophane, assorted curling ribbons, wired gold star garland, metallic confetti, gold glitter dimensional paint, champagne party popper, noisemaker, and craft glue (if needed).

1. Use gold paint to write "Happy New Year!" on front of bag.

2. For bag of confetti, place a handful of confetti at center of cellophane. Gather cellophane around confetti. Tie a length of ribbon into a bow around gathered cellophane; curl ends. Trim edges of cellophane.
3. Place gift in lunch bag.
4. Tie remaining ribbon lengths into a bow around bag; curl ends. Hold confetti bag close to top of lunch bag and wrap a length of star garland around both bags. Curl ends of garland around a pencil.
5. Place party popper and noisemaker inside top of bag; if necessary, glue to secure.

VALENTINE'S DAY CARAMELS

Give sweets to the sweet on Valentine's Day with these chewy caramel confections! Made with crisp rice cereal, butterscotch morsels, and candy coating, these treats will become a fast favorite. Our spray-painted doily gift sack features an organdy bow and a handcrafted tag.

BUTTERSCOTCH-CARAMEL CHEWIES

- 1 package (14 ounces) caramels
- 3 tablespoons water
- 1^1/$_2$ cups coarsely chopped pecans
- 1 cup coarsely crushed crispy rice cereal
- 6 ounces butterscotch chips
- 6 ounces vanilla candy coating
- 2 teaspoons vegetable shortening

Place caramels and water in the top of a double boiler over simmering water. Stir until caramels melt. Remove from heat and stir in pecans and cereal. Drop rounded teaspoons of mixture onto a baking sheet lined with lightly greased waxed paper.

In a heavy medium saucepan, melt butterscotch chips, candy coating, and shortening over low heat. Remove from heat (if butterscotch mixture begins to harden, return to heat). Dip candies in butterscotch mixture; place on waxed paper. Chill until set. Store in an airtight container in a cool place.

Yield: about 5^1/$_2$ dozen candies (5 gifts)

"LACY" PAPER BAG

For each bag, you will need a white lunch bag, 8" dia. paper doily, pink spray paint, floral-motif sticker for tag, pink felt-tip pen with medium point, ^{1}/$_2$ yd each of ^{3}/$_4$"w white and pink sheer ribbons, ^{1}/$_4$" hole punch, newspaper, and white tissue paper to line bag.

1. Place flattened bag front side up on newspaper.
2. Center doily on bag with doily extending about ^{1}/$_2$" beyond bottom of bag.
3. Lightly spray paint front of bag pink; remove doily.
4. Trim top edge of bag close to edges of stenciled doily.
5. For tag, cut a 1^3/$_4$" x 3^1/$_4$" paper piece with rounded corners from cut-away portion of bag. Adhere sticker to tag. Use pink pen to write "Happy Valentine's Day" on tag. Punch a hole in 1 corner of tag and near top of bag. Thread ribbon lengths through holes and tie into a bow; trim ends.
6. Line bag with tissue paper.

*S*urprise all your valentines with these dainty Cocoa Lace Cookies enveloped in little Victorian-look bags. The chocolaty confections will let each one know that someone thinks he or she is an angel! These beautiful bags are easy to make — just fold calendar pictures and glue the edges together!

COCOA LACE COOKIES

COOKIES

- $1/2$ cup butter or margarine, softened
- $1/3$ cup vegetable shortening
- 2 cups sugar
- 1 cup sour cream
- 2 eggs
- $1^1/2$ tablespoons vanilla extract
- $4^3/4$ cups all-purpose flour
- $1/2$ cup cocoa
- 1 tablespoon ground cinnamon
- 2 teaspoons baking powder
- 1 teaspoon baking soda
- $3/4$ teaspoon salt

ICING

- 2 tablespoons vegetable shortening
- 2 tablespoons butter or margarine, softened
- $1/2$ teaspoon vanilla extract
- 1 cup sifted confectioners sugar
- 2 teaspoons water

For cookies, cream butter, shortening, and sugar in a large bowl until fluffy. Add sour cream, eggs, and vanilla; beat until smooth. In a second large bowl, combine flour, cocoa, cinnamon, baking powder, baking soda, and salt. Add half of dry ingredients to creamed mixture; stir until a soft dough forms. Stir remaining dry ingredients, 1 cup at a time, into dough; use hands if necessary to mix well. Divide dough into fourths. Wrap in plastic wrap and chill 4 hours or until dough is firm.

Preheat oven to 350 degrees. On a lightly floured surface, use a floured rolling pin to roll out one fourth of dough to slightly less than $1/4$-inch thickness. Use a 4-inch scalloped heart-shaped and a 3-inch scalloped square cookie cutter to cut out cookies. Transfer to a greased baking sheet. Use aspic cutters, plastic straws, and/or a $1^1/4$-inch heart-shaped cookie cutter to make decorative cutouts in cookies. Bake 8 to 10 minutes or until firm to touch. Transfer cookies to a wire rack to cool. Repeat with remaining dough.

For icing, beat shortening, butter, and vanilla in a small bowl until fluffy. Add confectioners sugar and water; beat until smooth. Spoon icing into a pastry bag fitted with a small round tip. Pipe icing onto cookies. Allow icing to harden. Store in an airtight container.

Yield: about 4 dozen cookies (24 gifts)

CALENDAR BAG

For each bag, you will need an approx. 12" square cut from a decorative calendar page, a small motif cut from another calendar page, $1/2$ yd of 1"w wired ribbon, transparent tape, and a hot glue gun and glue sticks.

1. Fold calendar page as shown in Fig. 1.

Fig. 1

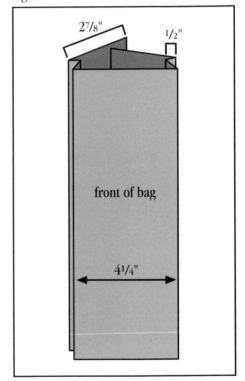

2. Overlap side edges at back of bag and glue together.
3. Fold bottom of bag $1/2$" to back; repeat and glue in place.
4. Tie ribbon into a bow; trim ends. Glue bow to front of bag about $1^1/2$" below top edge. Glue cut-out motif to bow.
5. Place gift in bag. Fold top of bag about $1^1/4$" to back; tape to secure.

A confection from Cupid, our creamy Peanut Butter-Molasses Fudge makes a sweet treat for a group of special people. Your friends will fall in love with the rich combination of flavors, and they'll adore your pretty gift bags, too! Each gold-accented sack and tag is stamped with flowers, then shaded with colored pencils. Delicate paper doilies and gold charms complete these gifts from the heart.

PEANUT BUTTER-MOLASSES FUDGE

3 cups firmly packed brown sugar
3/4 cup evaporated milk
1/2 cup molasses
3 tablespoons all-purpose flour
3/4 cup crunchy peanut butter, divided
1/2 cup butter or margarine
1 1/2 teaspoons vanilla extract
1 package (6 ounces) semisweet chocolate chips

Line a 9-inch square baking pan with aluminum foil, extending foil over 2 sides of pan; grease foil. Butter sides of a heavy large saucepan. Combine brown sugar, evaporated milk, molasses, and flour in saucepan. Stirring constantly, cook over medium-low heat until sugar dissolves. Using a pastry brush dipped in hot water, wash down any sugar crystals on sides of pan. Attach a candy thermometer to pan, making sure thermometer does not touch bottom of pan. Increase heat to medium and bring to a boil. Cook, without stirring, until mixture reaches 244 degrees or until 1/2 teaspoon of mixture will roll into a firm ball in ice water but will flatten if pressed when removed from the water. Remove from heat. Place pan in 2 inches of cold water in sink. Add 1/2 cup peanut butter, butter, and vanilla; do not stir. Cool to approximately 110 degrees. Remove from sink. Using medium speed of an electric mixer, beat until fudge thickens and begins to lose its gloss. Pour into prepared pan. Stirring constantly, melt chocolate chips and remaining 1/4 cup peanut butter in a heavy small saucepan over medium-low heat. Spread over fudge; chill 2 hours.

Cut fudge into 1-inch squares. Store in an airtight container in refrigerator.

Yield: about 6 1/2 dozen pieces fudge (4 gifts)

GILDED ROMANTIC BAG

For each bag, you will need a white lunch bag, an approx. 1"h rubber stamp with flower design, black ink pad, colored pencils, a 1 3/4" x 2 7/8" piece of cream-colored paper for tag, gold spray paint, Design Master® Glossy Wood Tone spray, gold dimensional paint, gold paint pen, 4" dia. white paper doily, 1 1/2"w gold heart-shaped charm, ruler, and a hot glue gun and glue sticks.

1. Use ruler and a pencil to draw a line around front and sides of bag 9" from bottom. Cut front and sides from bag above drawn line (Fig. 1).

Fig. 1

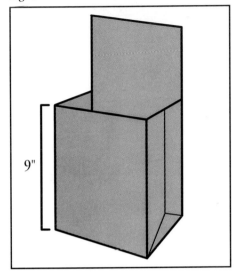

2. For flap, lay flattened bag on its front. Center a saucer upside down at top of bag and draw around edge of saucer closest to opening of bag. Cut bag along drawn line.
3. Spray paint back of bag and flap gold.
4. Use flower stamp and ink pad to stamp flowers on front of bag. Stamp a flower on 1 corner of paper piece for tag. Use colored pencils to color stamped flowers.
5. Lightly spray front of bag and doily with gold paint. Lightly spray front of bag and tag with wood tone spray.
6. Fold flap to front of bag. Use dimensional paint to paint gold dots on front of bag and to paint a decorative line along curved edge of flap.
7. Gather doily at center and glue to flap. Glue charm to doily.
8. For tag, use paint pen to write name and paint dots on tag. Glue tag to bag.

Tell your sweetie that you care with a batch of "Be Mine" Valentine Cookies presented in a heartwarming bag. The cute cookies, which resemble conversation heart candies, say it all with style and ease! The fanciful gift sack offers a window to the heart with its lace and doily trims.

"BE MINE" VALENTINE COOKIES

COOKIES

3/4	cup butter or margarine, softened
1	cup sifted confectioners sugar
1	egg
1	teaspoon vanilla extract
1	teaspoon butter flavoring
2 1/2	cups all-purpose flour
1/4	teaspoon salt
	Red, green, and yellow liquid food coloring

ICING

1	cup sifted confectioners sugar
1	tablespoon butter or margarine, softened
1/2	tablespoon vegetable shortening
2	teaspoons milk
1/4	teaspoon vanilla extract
1/4	teaspoon butter flavoring
1 1/4	teaspoons red liquid food coloring

For cookies, cream butter and confectioners sugar in a large bowl until fluffy. Add egg, vanilla, and butter flavoring; beat until smooth. In a medium bowl, combine flour and salt. Add dry ingredients to creamed mixture; stir until well blended. Divide dough into thirds; tint pink, light green, and yellow. Wrap in plastic wrap and chill 1 hour.

Preheat oven to 350 degrees. On a lightly floured surface, use a floured rolling pin to roll out one third of dough to 1/4-inch thickness. Use a 3-inch-wide heart-shaped cookie cutter to cut out cookies. Transfer to a greased baking sheet. Bake 8 to 10 minutes or until bottoms are lightly browned. Transfer cookies to a wire rack to cool. Repeat with remaining dough.

For icing, combine confectioners sugar, butter, shortening, milk, vanilla, and butter flavoring in a small bowl; beat until smooth. Stir in food coloring. Spoon icing into a pastry bag fitted with a small round tip. Pipe valentine messages onto cookies. Allow icing to harden. Store in an airtight container.

Yield: about 2 dozen cookies (2 gifts)

SWEETHEART BAG

For each bag, you will need a medium-size gift bag, 6" square of clear cellophane, colored paper for tag, three 1 3/4"w lace heart appliqués, 20" of 3/8"w lace trim, 3/4 yd of 2 1/2"w flat lace, 3/4 yd each of five assorted ribbons, candy conversation hearts, tracing paper, craft knife and small cutting mat or folded newspaper, a 1/8" hole punch, craft glue, and a hot glue gun and glue sticks.

1. Trace heart pattern, page 108, onto tracing paper; cut out. Use a pencil to draw around pattern at center front of bag. Place cutting mat inside front of bag and use craft knife to cut out heart along drawn lines.
2. Center cellophane square over heart opening on inside of bag; use craft glue to glue in place.
3. Beginning at bottom point of heart and mitering lace at center top of heart, hot glue 3/8"w lace trim to bag along edges of heart.
4. Hot glue 2 heart appliqués and several candy hearts to bag.
5. Tie 2 1/2"w lace into a bow; trim ends. Hot glue bow to bag. Tie ribbon lengths together into a bow; trim ends. Hot glue ribbon bow to lace bow.
6. For tag, glue remaining heart appliqué to paper. Cutting close to edges of appliqué, cut appliqué from paper. Hot glue 1 candy heart to center of tag. Punch a hole in top of tag. Thread tag onto 1 ribbon streamer. Knot streamer behind tag.

MILLIONAIRE PIE

You'll create more enchantment than a leprechaun on St. Patrick's Day when you share a gift of mouth-watering Millionaire Pie! Nestled in a shamrock-print fabric gift bag, this dessert is better than a pot of gold!

MILLIONAIRE PIES

    2 cans (8¹/₄ ounces each) crushed
         pineapple in heavy syrup
    1 egg white
    2 9-inch unbaked pie crusts
 1¹/₂ cups granulated sugar
    2 tablespoons all-purpose flour
  ¹/₂ cup butter or margarine, melted
    4 eggs
  ¹/₂ cup buttermilk
    2 cups whipping cream
    1 cup sifted confectioners sugar
  ³/₄ cup chopped pecans, toasted

Preheat oven to 350 degrees. Chill a medium bowl and beaters from an electric mixer in freezer. Reserving syrup, drain pineapple well; set aside. In a small bowl, lightly beat egg white. Lightly brush bottoms of pie crusts with egg white; chill until ready to fill. In a large bowl, combine sugar and flour. Pour melted butter over dry ingredients; stir until well blended. Add eggs, 1 at a time, beating well after each addition. Stir in buttermilk and ¹/₄ cup reserved pineapple syrup. Pour filling into pie crusts. Bake in bottom one-fourth of oven 25 to 30 minutes or until filling is set. If edges of crust brown too quickly, cover with a strip of aluminum foil. Cool pies on a wire rack 1 hour. Cover and chill 2 hours.

While beating whipping cream in chilled bowl, gradually add confectioners sugar; beat until stiff peaks form. Fold pineapple and pecans into whipped cream. Spread over chilled pie. Cover and store in refrigerator.

Yield: two 9-inch pies, about 8 servings each

ST. PATRICK'S DAY BAG

For each bag, you will need a 34" x 48" piece of shamrock-print fabric for bag, ¹/₂"w paper-backed fusible web tape, a 10" x 10" x 5" cake box, 30" of 1"w wired gold mesh ribbon, 22" of metallic gold twisted cord, assorted chocolate coins in gold wrappers, a purchased 1¹/₂" x 3³/₄" white gift tag with gold edging, green felt-tip pen with medium point, ¹/₄" hole punch, and a low-temperature hot glue gun and glue sticks.

1. For bag, follow Steps 2 - 4 of *Making a Fused Fabric Bag*, page 122.
2. Place pie in box; place box in bag.
3. To square bottom of bag, fold and glue corners of bag to bottom.
4. Glue coins to bag.
5. Tie ribbon into a bow around top of bag; trim ends.
6. Use green pen to write message and draw shamrocks on tag. Punch a hole in tag. Thread cord through hole. Tie cord into a bow around top of bag. Knot and fray ends of cord.

Easter "Egg-stravaganza"

*P*lay Easter Bunny for friends or co-workers with bags of our quick Easter Snack Mix! With a little fused-on fabric, ribbon, and buttons, you can make "egg-stravagant" bags in a jiffy.

Easter Snack Mix

- 2 packages (16 ounces each) pastel candy-coated chocolate-covered peanuts
- 2 packages (7 ounces each) milk chocolate candies covered with non-pareils
- 1 package (14 ounces) chocolate-covered raisins

In a large bowl, combine peanuts, chocolate candies, and chocolate-covered raisins. Cover and store in an airtight container.

Yield: about 8 cups snack mix (5 gifts)

Easter Egg Bags

For each bag, you will need a small gift bag; fabric(s) for egg; paper-backed fusible web; poster board; assorted decorative ribbons, trims, and buttons; tracing paper; and a hot glue gun and glue sticks.

1. Follow manufacturer's instructions to fuse web to wrong side of a 6" x 7" fabric piece. Remove paper backing; fuse fabric to poster board.
2. Trace egg pattern, page 108, onto tracing paper; cut out. Use pattern to cut egg from fabric-covered poster board.

3. For a fabric strip on egg, fuse web to wrong side of a 1¼" x 6" fabric strip. Remove paper backing; center and fuse strip across front of egg. Either trim strip even with edges of egg or fold ends of strip to back of egg and fuse in place.
4. Glue ribbons, bows tied from ribbons, trims, and buttons to egg as desired.
5. Glue egg to bag.

ARTY EASTER COOKIES

Children will love finding our spunky bunny bag on Easter morning — and the yummy treats hidden inside! The unique bag is created in minutes by dressing up a white lunch sack with a pom-pom, faux jewels, chenille stems, and other basic craft items. The buttery Easter Egg Cookies can be painted with swirls, polka dots, or zigzags using paste food coloring.

EASTER EGG COOKIES

- ½ cup butter or margarine, softened
- ½ cup sugar
- 1 egg
- ½ teaspoon vanilla extract
- ¼ teaspoon lemon extract
- 1⅔ cups all-purpose flour
- ½ teaspoon baking powder
- ¼ teaspoon salt
  Pink, violet, and yellow paste food coloring

Cream butter and sugar in a large bowl until fluffy. Add egg and extracts; beat until smooth. In a small bowl, combine flour, baking powder, and salt. Add dry ingredients to creamed mixture; stir until well blended. Wrap dough in plastic wrap and chill 1 hour.

Preheat oven to 350 degrees. On a lightly floured surface, use a floured rolling pin to roll out dough to ⅛-inch thickness. Use a 1½ x 2½-inch egg-shaped cookie cutter to cut out cookies. Transfer to a lightly greased baking sheet. Bake 7 to 9 minutes or until bottoms are lightly browned. Transfer cookies to a wire rack to cool.

Place 1 teaspoon of water in each of 3 small bowls; tint dark pink, violet, and yellow. Paint desired designs on cookies; allow to dry. Store in an airtight container.

Yield: about 4½ dozen cookies (3 gifts)

BUNNY BAG

For each bag, you will need a white lunch bag, white paper for teeth, pink felt for cheeks, 1½" dia. pink pom-pom for nose, 3 purple chenille stems for whiskers, two 9mm blue acrylic jewels for eyes, ½ yd of 1½"w wired ribbon, 6" of white twisted paper, black felt-tip pen with medium point, 3" of floral wire, tracing paper, and a hot glue gun and glue sticks.

1. To fringe top of bag, make 2" long cuts about every ¼" along top edge of flattened bag.
2. Trace teeth and cheek patterns onto tracing paper; cut out. Use patterns to cut teeth from white paper and 2 cheeks from felt.
3. Use black pen to draw along outer edges of teeth; draw a line at center to separate teeth. Glue teeth to center of bag about 3" from bottom.
4. For whiskers and nose, cut an 8" length from each chenille stem. Glue centers of stems to pom-pom. Glue whiskers and nose to bag. Arrange whiskers as desired.
5. Glue cheeks to bag. For eyes, glue jewels to bag above nose.
6. Place gift in bag. Twist top of bag closed; secure with wire just below fringe. Tie ribbon into a bow around bag, covering wire; trim ends.
7. For ears, untwist twisted paper; cutting with grain of paper, cut paper in half. Twist ends of each paper length. Glue 1 end of 1 paper length to each side of bag at fold.

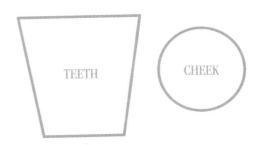

TEETH   CHEEK

EASY EASTER HAM

*G*randa may have outgrown the Easter Bunny, but she'll still appreciate a time-saving gift of glazed ham! For a beautiful presentation, deliver a ham and a jar of glaze in a bag graced with a cheery springtime bouquet. The recipe makes enough glaze for two gifts.

EASTER HAM GLAZE

- 2 cans (20 ounces each) crushed pineapple, drained
- 2 cups firmly packed brown sugar
- 1/4 cup honey
- 1 tablespoon dry mustard
- 1 teaspoon ground cloves
- 2 fully-cooked boneless hams (4 to 5 pounds each) to give with glaze

In a heavy large saucepan, combine pineapple, brown sugar, honey, dry mustard, and cloves. Stirring frequently, cook over medium heat about 5 minutes or until sugar dissolves. Cook about 10 minutes or until liquid reduces and mixture thickens. Remove from heat and allow to cool.

Store in an airtight container in refrigerator. Give with serving instructions.

Yield: about 4 1/4 cups glaze (2 gifts)

To serve: Preheat oven to 325 degrees. Score surface of ham in a diamond pattern. Insert a meat thermometer into center of ham. Cover and bake 1 hour. Uncover ham; spoon glaze over ham.

Spooning glaze over ham every 15 minutes, bake 45 minutes to 1 hour or until thermometer registers 140 degrees.

Yield: about 16 servings

EASTER BOUQUET BAG

You will need a grocery bag, fabric to cover bag, paper-backed fusible web, bouquet of spring silk flowers, 25" of 2 1/2"w wired sheer white ribbon, 25" of 2 1/4"w white satin ribbon, one 1 3/8" x 2 3/8" piece each of white and colored paper, shredded paper to line bag (available at craft and party supply stores), black felt-tip pen with medium point, wire cutters (if needed), and a hot glue gun and glue sticks.

1. Cut 6" from top of bag; discard.
2. Follow manufacturer's instructions to fuse web to wrong side of fabric.
3. Cut a piece of fabric same size as front of bag; remove paper backing. Fuse fabric to bag.
4. For cuff, fold top edge of bag down about 1 3/4"; repeat.
5. Flatten bouquet slightly and arrange flowers in a fan shape. Tie ribbon lengths together into a bow around bouquet stem. If necessary, use wire cutters to trim bouquet stem. Glue bouquet to bag.
6. For tag, use black pen to write "Happy Easter" on white paper piece. Glue white paper piece to colored paper piece. Glue tag to bag.
7. Line bag with shredded paper.

TAKE-A-BREAK MUFFINS

*O*n Secretary's Day, encourage your tireless assistant to take a well-deserved break. Our moist Lemon-Pecan Muffins are fast to make, and they're especially tasty when enjoyed with a cup of coffee or tea! For a personal touch, embellish the gift bag with a handwritten memo.

LEMON-PECAN MUFFINS

- $1/2$ cup butter or margarine, softened
- $1/2$ cup plus 2 tablespoons sugar
- 2 eggs
- 1 teaspoon vanilla extract
- 1 teaspoon lemon extract
- 1 teaspoon freshly grated lemon zest
- $1/2$ cup all-purpose flour
- $1/2$ teaspoon baking powder
- $1/8$ teaspoon salt
- 2 cups finely chopped pecans

Preheat oven to 325 degrees. Line a muffin pan with paper muffin cups. In a medium bowl, cream butter and sugar until fluffy. Add eggs, extracts, and lemon zest; beat until well blended. In a small bowl, combine flour, baking powder, and salt. Add dry ingredients to creamed mixture; stir until just moistened. Stir in pecans. Fill muffin cups about two-thirds full. Bake 25 to 30 minutes or until a toothpick inserted in center of muffin comes out clean. Serve warm or cool completely on a wire rack. Store in an airtight container.

Yield: about 1 dozen muffins (2 gifts)

SECRETARY'S DAY BAG

For each bag, you will need a medium-size gift bag, steno pad page, assorted curling ribbons and felt-tip pens to coordinate with bag, an old felt-tip pen without cap for decoration on bag, tissue paper to line bag, craft glue stick, and a hot glue gun and glue sticks.

1. Use felt-tip pens to write message on steno pad page.

2. Use glue stick to glue page to front of bag.

3. Hot glue old pen to bag.

4. Form a multi-loop bow from several lengths of curling ribbon, tying bow at center with another length of ribbon; curl ends. Hot glue bow to bag.

5. Line bag with tissue paper.

MOTHER'S TEATIME FAVORITES

*T*he gifts Mom loves the best are prepared with your own hands — so surprise her on her special day with Cinnamon-Orange Biscotti! Place the crunchy teatime favorites in a cheerful gift bag adorned with a teapot magnet for a gift that echoes "Happy Mother's Day!" all year long.

CINNAMON-ORANGE BISCOTTI

- ¹/₂ cup butter or margarine, softened
- 1 cup sugar
- 3 eggs
- 1 tablespoon grated orange zest
- 1 teaspoon orange extract
- 3 cups all-purpose flour
- 1 teaspoon baking powder
- ¹/₂ teaspoon baking soda
- ¹/₂ teaspoon ground cinnamon
- ¹/₈ teaspoon salt

Preheat oven to 375 degrees. In a large bowl, cream butter and sugar until fluffy. Add eggs, orange zest, and orange extract; beat until smooth. In a medium bowl, combine flour, baking powder, baking soda, cinnamon, and salt. Add dry ingredients to creamed mixture; stir until a soft dough forms. Divide dough in half. On a greased and floured baking sheet, shape each piece of dough into a 2¹/₂ x 10-inch loaf, flouring hands as necessary. Allow 3 inches between loaves on baking sheet. Bake 25 to 28 minutes or until loaves are lightly browned; cool 10 minutes on baking sheet. Cut loaves diagonally into ¹/₂-inch slices. Place slices flat on an ungreased baking sheet. Bake about 7 minutes or until lightly browned.

Turn slices over and bake 6 to 8 minutes longer or until lightly browned. Transfer cookies to a wire rack to cool. Store in a cookie tin.

Yield: about 2¹/₂ dozen cookies (2 gifts)

MOTHER'S DAY BAG

For each bag, you will need a medium-size gift bag with handles; white Bristol board; colored paper for banner; 1¹/₈ yds of 1¹/₄"w grosgrain ribbon; 22" of 2"w sheer ribbon; two 2" lengths of self-adhesive magnetic tape; white, green, black, and assorted colors of acrylic paint; small paintbrushes; black felt-tip pen with fine point; tracing paper; graphite transfer paper; floral wire; tissue paper to line bag; and a hot glue gun and glue sticks.

1. Trace teapot and banner patterns, page 109, onto tracing paper. Use transfer paper to transfer teapot design to Bristol board and banner design to colored paper; cut out. Paint teapot as desired (we used a paintbrush handle dipped in paint to paint dots on our teapot).
2. Adhere 1 piece of magnetic strip to back of teapot. Adhere remaining strip to bag. Attach teapot to bag.
3. Use black pen to write "Happy Mother's Day!" on banner. Glue banner to bag.
4. Follow *Making a Multi-Loop Bow,* page 123, to form a bow with grosgrain ribbon. Tie sheer ribbon into a bow around handle of bag and center of multi-loop bow; trim ends.
5. Line bag with tissue paper.

MILADY'S APRICOT CANDIES

*W*hether she's your mother, grandmother, aunt, or just a good friend, she'll adore a gift of yummy Apricot Candies! On Mother's Day, present these fruity no-bake confections in pretty bags adorned with printed paper napkins, silk roses, and matching tags.

APRICOT CANDIES

- 1 package (14 ounces) flaked coconut
- 1 cup plus 3 tablespoons slivered almonds, divided
- 1 can (14 ounces) sweetened condensed milk
- 1¹/₂ cups sifted confectioners sugar
- 2 packages (3 ounces each) apricot gelatin, divided
- ¹/₂ teaspoon almond extract
- 1¹/₂ teaspoons water
- 5 drops liquid green food coloring
  Paper candy cups and small green silk leaves to decorate

Process coconut and 1 cup slivered almonds in food processor until finely ground. In a medium bowl, combine coconut mixture, sweetened condensed milk, confectioners sugar, 1 package gelatin, and almond extract; mix until well blended. Cover and chill about 1¹/₂ hours or until firm enough to handle.

In a small bowl, combine water and food coloring. Add remaining 3 tablespoons slivered almonds; stir until well coated. Spread tinted almonds on paper towels to dry. Shape slightly rounded teaspoonfuls of candy into balls

to resemble apricots. In a small bowl, roll balls in remaining gelatin. Make an indentation in one end of each candy and press a green almond into indentation for stem. Place on a baking sheet; chill until firm. Place candies in paper candy cups and decorate with leaves; store in refrigerator.

Yield: about 5¹/₂ dozen candies (7 gifts)

NAPKIN-COVERED BAG

For each bag, you will need a white lunch bag, a large printed paper napkin (our napkin measured 6¹/₂" square when folded), ¹/₂ yd each of 1¹/₂"w and 2"w sheer ribbon, 7" of gold cord, silk rose with leaves, 3¹/₂" x 5¹/₂" white paper piece for tag, tissue paper to line bag, ¹/₈" hole punch, spray adhesive, and a hot glue gun and glue sticks.

1. Unfold and press napkin. Separate napkin into layers. Discard all but printed layer of napkin.
2. Use spray adhesive to carefully glue printed napkin layer to front of flattened bag. Trim napkin layer even with edges of bag. Set aside remainder of napkin layer.
3. Tie ribbon lengths together into a bow; trim ends. Hot glue bow to bag. Hot glue rose to bow.
4. For tag, use spray adhesive to glue remainder of printed napkin layer to white paper piece. Trim napkin layer even with edges of paper piece. Matching short edges, fold tag in half with napkin-covered side out. Punch a hole in tag. Thread cord through hole and 1 loop of bow and knot ends together; trim and fray ends.
5. Line bag with tissue paper.

You'll reel in the compliments when you surprise Dad with this fun fish-fry kit! The handy sponge-painted tote is packed with our Favorite Fish-Fry Seasoning — a spicy coating with paprika, parsley, and red pepper — and a bag of ready-to-make Hush Puppy Mix. What a delicious way to catch his attention on Father's Day!

FAVORITE FISH-FRY SEASONING

2 cups yellow cornmeal
1 cup all-purpose flour
2 teaspoons paprika
1 teaspoon dried parsley flakes, crushed
1 teaspoon salt
1 teaspoon celery salt
1 teaspoon onion salt
1 teaspoon lemon pepper
1/2 teaspoon ground red pepper

In a large bowl, combine cornmeal, flour, paprika, parsley, salt, celery salt, onion salt, lemon pepper, and red pepper. Store in a resealable plastic bag. Give with serving instructions.

Yield: about 3 cups mix (will coat about 4 pounds of fish)

To serve: Heat about 1 1/2 inches vegetable oil to 375 degrees in a deep skillet. In a small bowl, combine 1 egg and 1 cup buttermilk. Dip fish into buttermilk mixture. Place in bag of mix; shake until fish is well coated. Fry until fish is golden brown and flakes easily with a fork. Drain on paper towels. Serve warm.

HUSH PUPPY MIX

1 1/2 cups yellow cornmeal
3/4 cup all-purpose flour
3 tablespoons dried minced onion
1 teaspoon baking powder
1 teaspoon sugar
1 teaspoon salt
1/2 teaspoon baking soda
1/4 teaspoon ground red pepper

In a large bowl, combine cornmeal, flour, onion, baking powder, sugar, salt, baking soda, and red pepper. Store in a resealable plastic bag. Give with serving instructions.

Yield: about 2 1/4 cups mix

To serve: Heat about 1 1/2 inches vegetable oil to 350 degrees in a deep skillet. In a medium bowl, combine 1 1/4 cups buttermilk, 1 beaten egg, and mix; stir until well blended. Drop mixture by tablespoonfuls into hot oil. Fry until golden brown and thoroughly cooked. Drain on paper towels. Serve warm.

Yield: about 3 dozen hush puppies

SPONGE-PAINTED FISH TOTE

You will need a canvas tote bag, 1 yd of 2 1/2"w wired net ribbon, a Miracle Sponge® (dry, compressed sponge available at craft stores), yellow and green acrylic paint, black dimensional paint, paper towels, tracing paper, and tissue paper to line bag.

1. Trace fish pattern onto tracing paper; cut out.
2. Use pattern to cut shape from dry sponge.
3. Using sponge shape and green and yellow paint, follow *Sponge Painting,* page 121, to paint fish on tote.
4. Use black paint to paint dots on fish for eyes.
5. Line tote with tissue paper.
6. Place gift in tote.
7. Tie ribbon into a bow around tote handles; trim ends.

A TOAST TO DAD

*O*n Father's Day, invite Dad to "sip" into something more comfortable with a bottle of home-brewed Coffee-Flavored Liqueur! The smooth beverage is a blend of vodka, coffee, and chocolate. Dad will be doubly delighted when he realizes that the new necktie decorating his gift bag is the second half of his special-day surprise!

COFFEE-FLAVORED LIQUEUR

Make this gift early to allow flavor to fully develop.

- 4 cups sugar
- 4 cups water
- 3/4 cup instant coffee granules
- 2 tablespoons chocolate syrup
- 1 vanilla bean, cut into fourths
- 1 bottle (750 ml) vodka

In a large saucepan, bring sugar and water to a boil over medium-high heat; boil 10 minutes. Remove from heat and cool.

Transfer sugar syrup to a 1-gallon container with lid. Stir in coffee granules, chocolate syrup, and vanilla bean pieces. Stir in vodka. Cover and allow flavor to develop 2 to 3 weeks, at room temperature, shaking or stirring once a day. Remove vanilla bean pieces before giving. Store in an airtight container in a cool place.

Yield: about 8 1/2 cups liqueur (1 gift)

FATHER'S DAY BAG

You will need a brown bottle bag, a necktie, two small white buttons, 2 large paper clips, white paper, and a hot glue gun and glue sticks.

1. Place gift in bag.
2. Tie necktie so that it measures same length as height of bag from top of knot to bottom of tie.
3. Place loop of necktie in bag. Use paper clips to clip top of bag closed.

4. For collar, trace collar pattern, page 109, onto white paper; cut out. Fold collar along fold line (indicated in grey on pattern). Glue side edges of collar together. Glue buttons to collar.
5. Place collar over top of bag and necktie. Glue back of collar to back of bag to secure.

STAR-SPANGLED SALAD

*W*ow the crowd at the next Fourth of July picnic with delicious Spinach Salad served with Cherry Vinaigrette! For this taste-tempter, fresh greens are tossed with slivered almonds and red onions, then drizzled with the sweet, tangy dressing. The star-spangled carrier has a simple fused-on fabric front and is decorated with a miniature flag.

SPINACH SALAD WITH CHERRY VINAIGRETTE

CHERRY VINAIGRETTE
- 1 cup frozen dark sweet cherries
- 1/2 cup orange juice
- 1 tablespoon sugar
- 2 tablespoons vegetable oil
- 1 tablespoon balsamic vinegar
- 1/8 teaspoon ground ginger
- 1/8 teaspoon salt
- 1/8 teaspoon ground black pepper

SALAD
- 12 cups washed, stemmed, dried, and torn spinach leaves
- 1 small red onion, thinly sliced and separated into rings
- 3/4 cup slivered almonds, toasted

For cherry vinaigrette, process cherries and orange juice in a food processor until cherries are finely chopped. Combine cherry mixture and sugar in a small saucepan over medium heat. Stirring frequently, cook about 3 minutes or until sugar dissolves. Remove from heat; stir in oil, vinegar, ginger, salt, and pepper. Transfer vinaigrette to an airtight

container. Let stand at room temperature 2 hours to allow flavors to develop.

For salad, place spinach and onion in a 1-gallon resealable plastic bag; store in refrigerator. Place slivered almonds in a small resealable plastic bag.

Yield: about 12 servings (1 gift)

PATRIOTIC BAG AND JAR

You will need a grocery bag, fabric to cover bag and jar lid, paper-backed fusible web, curling ribbons, lightweight cardboard, small American flag, and a hot glue gun and glue sticks.

1. Follow manufacturer's instructions to fuse web to wrong side of fabric to cover bag.
2. Cut a piece of fabric same size as front of bag; remove paper backing. Fuse fabric to bag.
3. For cuff, fold top edge of bag down about 2"; repeat.
4. Tie several lengths of curling ribbon into a bow around flagpole; curl ribbon ends. Glue flag to bag.
5. Follow *Jar Lid Finishing*, page 122, omitting batting, to finish jar lid.

*T*ry this revolutionary approach to help a class of American History students get into the spirit of learning! Pass out bags of Yankee-Noodle Snack Mix, complete with a feather stuck in each folded-paper hat. The sweet, crunchy treat is extra-easy to stir together using simple ingredients. Sprinkled with honey-roasted almonds and red and blue jelly beans, this dandy snack has a taste worth celebrating!

YANKEE-NOODLE SNACK MIX

  2 packages (12 ounces each) chow mein noodles
  2 cups dried coconut chips
  1 can (6 ounces) honey-roasted whole almonds
20 ounces vanilla candy coating
  8 ounces *each* red and blue small gourmet jelly beans

In a large roasting pan, combine chow mein noodles, coconut chips, and almonds. In a heavy medium saucepan, melt candy coating over low heat. Pour over noodle mixture; stir gently until well coated. Spread on lightly greased aluminum foil to let candy coating harden. Add jelly beans. Store in an airtight container.

Yield: about 25 cups snack mix (25 gifts)

YANKEE-NOODLE BAG

For each bag, you will need a penny sack, a 6" x 8¹/₂" piece of newspaper, an approx. 5" long white feather, 12" of ⁵/₈"w patriotic ribbon, stapler, and a hot glue gun and glue sticks.

1. Place gift in bag.
2. Fold top of bag about 1" to back; staple closed.
3. Matching short edges, fold newspaper piece in half. Place fold at top. Referring to Fig. 1, fold 1 top corner of folded newspaper piece diagonally just past center.

Fig. 1

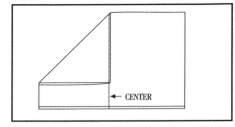

4. Fold remaining top corner diagonally over first folded corner (Fig. 2).

Fig. 2

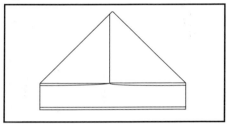

5. Fold bottom edges up at front and back for brim (Fig. 3).

Fig. 3

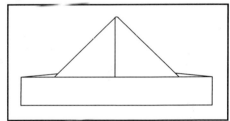

6. Place hat over top of bag; staple at center of brim to secure.
7. Tie ribbon into a bow; trim ends. Glue feather and bow to hat over staple.

*G*randparents' Day (the first Sunday after Labor Day) gives us a wonderful opportunity to celebrate our grandparents and let them know how greatly they've influenced our lives. Packed with a moist, buttery Whipping Cream Pound Cake, our family photos gift bag is sure to prompt memories of special family moments. The unique carrier is covered with photocopies of favorite snapshots and handwritten messages from the children and grandchildren.

WHIPPING CREAM POUND CAKE

 1 cup butter, softened
 3 cups sugar
 6 eggs
 3 cups plus 3 tablespoons sifted
   cake flour
 1 cup whipping cream
 1 teaspoon vanilla extract

Do not preheat oven. Grease and flour a heavy 10-inch fluted tube pan. In a large bowl, cream butter and sugar until fluffy. Add eggs, 1 at a time, beating thoroughly after each addition. Alternately beat cake flour and whipping cream into creamed mixture until well blended. Stir in vanilla. Pour batter into prepared pan. Place pan in cold oven and set temperature at 300 degrees. Bake 1 hour 15 minutes to 1 hour 40 minutes or until a toothpick inserted in center of cake comes out clean. Cool in pan 10 minutes. Invert cake onto a serving plate; cool completely. Store in an airtight container.

Yield: about 16 servings

FAMILY PHOTOS GIFT BAG

You will need a grocery bag, black and white photocopies of family photographs and decorative paper(s), parchment paper, two 7/8" dia. buttons, 20" of brown embroidery floss, Design Master® Glossy Wood Tone spray, stapler, assorted black felt-tip pens, craft glue stick, and a hot glue gun and glue sticks.

1. Place flattened bag front side-up with bottom of bag at top and opening at bottom.
2. Cut out photocopied photographs. Use glue stick to glue photograph cutouts to photocopies of decorative paper(s). Cutting about 3/4" from edges of photographs, cut out photographs. Lightly spray photocopies with wood tone spray.
3. Cut various sizes of rectangles from parchment paper. Have family members write messages on the paper pieces using black pens.
4. Use glue stick to glue photographs and messages to front of bag to within about 4" from opening edge.
5. Cut away top 4" of each side of bag. Staple a 3/4" pleat in each side of bag (Fig. 1).

Fig. 1

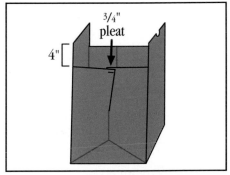

6. Fold corners of bottom flap diagonally toward center; use glue stick to secure (Fig. 2).

Fig. 2

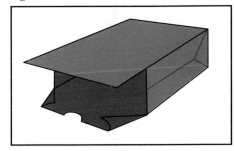

7. Hot glue 1 button to center of top flap at fold line. Hot glue remaining button to center of bottom flap close to edge.
8. Place gift in bag. Close bottom flap over top flap; wrap embroidery floss around buttons to secure.

A *trio of tempting toppings is included in this hearty Baked Potato Kit for National Boss Day! For this delicious surprise, a large grocery bag is simply covered with colorful kitchen towels and loaded with baking potatoes and crocks of garlic-pepper butter, bacon-cheddar topping, and low-fat salsa topping. What a tasty way to say, "You're the tops!"*

BAKED POTATO KIT

BACON-CHEDDAR TOPPING

   1 cup sour cream
 2/3 cup finely shredded Cheddar cheese
 1/2 cup cooked and crumbled bacon
   2 tablespoons finely chopped green onion

Yield: about 1 1/2 cups topping

GARLIC-PEPPER BUTTER

 1/2 cup butter, softened
   2 small cloves garlic, minced
 1 1/2 teaspoons freshly ground black pepper

Yield: about 1/2 cup topping

LOW-FAT SALSA TOPPING

 1/4 cup fat-free sour cream
 1/4 cup thick salsa
   2 tablespoons chopped ripe olives
   1 tablespoon finely chopped green onion

Yield: about 1/2 cup topping

   6 uncooked baking potatoes to give with toppings

In 3 small bowls, combine ingredients for each topping; stir until well blended. Cover and store in refrigerator. Give toppings with baking potatoes.

BOSS DAY GIFT BAG

You will need a brown grocery bag, 3 brown lunch bags, 2 approx. 20" x 27" kitchen towels, 2 large buttons, 3 medium-size buttons, embroidery floss, large needle, cream-colored and red paper, jute twine, black felt-tip pen with fine point, 1/4" hole punch, stapler, craft glue stick, and a hot glue gun and glue sticks.

1. Fold top of grocery bag down about 2"; repeat twice.
2. To cover bag, measure width of bag front. Place 1 towel wrong side up on ironing board; press long edges of towel to center so that towel is same width as bag front. Place bag across center of towel. Bring ends of towel up and fold to inside of bag. Staple towel at top edge to secure.
3. Use remaining towel to line bag, folding ends of towel to outside over top of bag for cuff.
4. For label on bag, cut a 2" x 9" strip of cream-colored paper. Use black pen to write "BAKED POTATO KIT" on paper strip. Use large needle and floss to sew label and large buttons to cuff of bag; knot floss at front of buttons and trim ends.
5. Place toppings in lunch bags. Tie a length of twine into a bow around top of each bag; trim ends. Hot glue 1 medium-size button to each bow.
6. For tags on lunch bags, cut three 1 1/2" x 3" pieces of cream-colored paper. Use black pen to write "bacon-cheddar topping," "garlic-pepper butter," and "low-fat salsa topping" on tags. Use glue stick to glue tags to red paper. Cutting close to each tag, cut tags from red paper. Punch a hole in each tag. Thread 1 tag onto 1 end of twine on each lunch bag. Knot twine to secure tag to bag.
7. Place potatoes and bags of toppings in gift bag.

JACK-O'-LANTERN PUNCH

There's no need to go to the pumpkin patch to find the perfect Halloween hostess gift — just pick our Spicy Jack-O'-Lantern Punch instead! Prepared with fruit juices and pumpkin pie spice, it's a fun, fizzy brew. The sponge-painted pumpkin bag can be refilled with paper for a cute holiday decoration.

SPICY JACK-O'-LANTERN PUNCH

1 can (12 ounces) frozen orange juice concentrate, thawed
1 can (12 ounces) frozen orange-pineapple juice concentrate, thawed
2 cups water
1 package (0.15 ounces) unsweetened orange-flavored soft drink mix
2 teaspoons pumpkin pie spice

In a 1¹/₂-quart container, combine juice concentrates and water. Add soft drink mix and pumpkin pie spice; whisk until well blended. Cover and chill. Give with serving instructions.

Yield: about 5 cups mix (1 gift)

To serve: Place punch mix in a 1-gallon container. Add four 12-ounce cans of chilled lemon-lime soft drink. Stir and serve immediately.

Yield: about 11 cups punch

PUMPKIN BAG

You will need a brown lunch bag, a 3" square of cream-colored paper, orange and dark orange acrylic paint, small sponge pieces, silk grape leaf sprig, natural raffia, brown felt-tip pen with fine point, paper towels, ¹/₈" hole punch, and newspaper.

1. Fill bag with crumpled newspaper.
2. Use sponge pieces and follow *Sponge Painting,* page 121, to paint outside of bag and just inside top edge of bag with orange, then dark orange paint.
3. Remove newspapers from bag. Place gift in bag.
4. Tie several lengths of raffia into a bow around top of bag; trim ends. Tuck grape leaf sprig behind bow.
5. For tag, use brown pen to write serving instructions (this page) on paper square. Punch hole in tag. Thread tag onto 1 tendril of grape leaf sprig.

HALLOWEEN TREATS

*H*alloween isn't just for kids, and our "deluxe" Halloween kits are great for getting adults into the mischievous spirit! The simple brown bags go incognito with purchased masks. But there's no disguising the great taste of our Peanut Butter Candy Bars — they're yummy treats that grown-up ghouls will be dying to sink their teeth into!

PEANUT BUTTER CANDY BARS

3³/₄ cups sifted confectioners sugar
3 cups cocoa-flavored crispy rice
    cereal
2 cups smooth peanut butter
¹/₂ cup butter or margarine
1 package (6 ounces) semisweet
    chocolate chips
6 ounces chocolate candy coating,
    cut into pieces

In a large bowl, combine confectioners sugar and cereal. In a medium microwave-safe bowl, combine peanut butter and butter. Microwave on medium-high power (80%) 2 minutes or until mixture melts, stirring after each minute. Pour peanut butter mixture over cereal mixture; stir until well blended. Press mixture into bottom of an ungreased 9 x 13-inch baking pan. In a medium microwave-safe bowl, combine chocolate chips and candy coating. Microwave on medium-high power (80%) 2 to 3 minutes or until mixture softens, stirring after each minute until smooth. Spread chocolate mixture over candy. Allow chocolate mixture to harden. Cut

into 1 x 2-inch bars. Store in an airtight container in a cool place.

Yield: about 4 dozen bars (4 gifts)

HALLOWEEN KIT BAG

For each bag, you will need a brown lunch bag, novelty glasses with nose, fluorescent orange dimensional paint, black felt-tip pen with medium point, and a ¹/₄" hole punch.

1. Use paint to write "HALLOWEEN KIT" on front of flattened bag. Use black pen to write "A COSTUME <u>AND</u> A TREAT!" on bag and draw arrow.
2. Place gift in bag.
3. Fold top of bag about 2" to front. Punch a hole close to top at each side of bag. Insert earpieces of novelty glasses through holes and fold at back.

33

These "boo-tiful" bags are a fun way to deliver happy Halloween wishes! The haunting holders are quickly crafted from white lunch sacks and packed with our spooky Spiderweb Cookies. Adorned with an icing web design and a candy spider, the chocolaty sweets are a "scream" come true!

SPIDERWEB COOKIES

COOKIES
- 1⅓ cups butter or margarine, softened
- 1⅓ cups sugar
- 2 eggs
- 1½ teaspoons vanilla extract
- 3⅓ cups all-purpose flour
- ⅓ cup cocoa

ICING AND SPIDERWEBS
- 4½ cups sifted confectioners sugar
- 1½ teaspoons vanilla extract
- ⅓ cup plus 1 teaspoon milk
- ½ cup semisweet chocolate chips
  Gummi spiders to decorate

Preheat oven to 350 degrees. For cookies, cream butter and sugar in a large bowl until fluffy. Add eggs and vanilla; beat until smooth. In a medium bowl, combine flour and cocoa. Add dry ingredients to creamed mixture; beat until well blended. Shape dough into thirty 1½-inch-diameter balls and place 2 inches apart on a lightly greased baking sheet; flatten balls into 3-inch circles with bottom of a lightly greased glass. Bake 9 to 11 minutes or until bottoms are lightly browned. Cool cookies on baking sheet 2 minutes; transfer to a wire rack to cool completely.

For icing, place confectioners sugar in a medium bowl; add vanilla and gradually stir in milk until icing is desired spreading consistency. Cover and set aside. Place chocolate chips in a small microwave-safe bowl. Microwave on high power (100%) 1 minute or until chocolate softens; stir until smooth. Spoon melted chocolate into a pastry bag fitted with a small round tip. Working with 2 cookies at a time, spread icing on cookies. Beginning at center of each cookie, pipe 3 or 4 chocolate circles, one outside the other and about ¼-inch apart, onto wet icing. Beginning at smallest circle, pull a toothpick through circles to outer edge of icing to make spiderweb design. Decorate cookies with candy spiders. Repeat with remaining cookies, icing, and chocolate. Allow icing to harden. Wrap cookies individually.

Yield: 30 cookies (3 gifts)

GHOST BAG

For each bag, you will need 2 white lunch bags; white, orange, and black paper; green raffia; black felt-tip pen with medium point; tracing paper; and a hot glue gun and glue sticks.

1. Trace patterns, page 110, onto tracing paper; cut out. Use patterns to cut feet from black paper, 2 hands from white paper, and pumpkin from orange paper.
2. Glue feet to bottom of 1 bag.
3. Make a fold in each hand about ½" from straight edge.
4. Use black pen to write "Boo!" on pumpkin. Tie several 12" lengths of raffia into a bow; trim ends. Glue bow to pumpkin.
5. Turn remaining bag upside down. Glue hands and pumpkin to second bag. Use black pen to draw eyes on bag.
6. Place gift in first bag. Twist top of bag closed and knot a 6" length of raffia around bag. Place second bag over top of first bag.

BEWITCHING SNACK

PUMPKIN WITCH AND "BOO" CAT BAGS

Little ghouls and goblins will love these bewitching yet easy-to-make goodie bags filled with Candy Pumpkin Snack Mix! Trick-or-treaters will howl for more of the tasty mix, which combines mini peanut butter sandwich crackers with candy pumpkins and chocolate-covered peanuts.

For each bag, you will need a small brown bag; orange, dark orange, and black acrylic paint; paintbrushes; tracing paper; and craft glue.

For each pumpkin witch bag, you will *also* need an approx. 6" dia. felt witch's hat, fabric for hatband, white and yellow acrylic paint, and graphite transfer paper.

For each "Boo" cat bag, you will *also* need yellow and black paper, black raffia, black felt-tip pen with fine point, and a ⅛" hole punch.

PUMPKIN WITCH BAG

1. Paint bag orange.
2. Trace witch face pattern, page 110, onto tracing paper. Use transfer paper to transfer pattern to bag.
3. Paint cheeks and lines at bottom of face dark orange. Paint mouth, nose, eyes, eyebrows, and outlines black. Paint tooth and highlights in eyes white. Highlight cheeks and lines at bottom of face with yellow.
4. For hatband, measure around crown of hat; add ½". Cut a 1"w fabric strip the determined length. With wrong sides together, press strip in half lengthwise.

Glue hatband around crown of hat, overlapping ends at back.
5. Place gift in bag. Twist top of bag closed and place hat on bag.

"BOO" CAT BAG

1. Paint bag orange. Paint dark orange and black stripes on bag to make plaid pattern.
2. Trace moon, cat, and "Boo" patterns onto tracing paper; cut out. Use patterns to cut moon from yellow paper and cat and "Boo" from black paper.
3. Glue cat to moon. Use black pen to draw dashed lines along edges of moon to resemble stitching.
4. Glue "Boo" to yellow paper. Cutting close to word, cut word from paper; glue to bag.
5. Place moon at top of flattened bag. Punch 2 holes through top of moon and bag.
6. Place gift in bag.
7. Thread a length of raffia through holes in moon and bag and tie into a bow at front of bag; trim ends.

CANDY PUMPKIN SNACK MIX

  1 package (10½ ounces) mini peanut butter sandwich crackers
16 ounces pumpkin-shaped candies
  1 package (7 ounces) chocolate-covered peanuts

In a large bowl, combine crackers, pumpkin candies, and chocolate-covered peanuts. Store in an airtight container.

Yield: about 8 cups snack mix (4 gifts)

A gift of savory Squash and Wild Rice Soup is ideal for sharing the blessing of a bountiful harvest at Thanksgiving. This nutritious blend features zucchini, yellow squash, and two kinds of rice in a well-seasoned chicken stock. For the unique tote, we decorated a purchased gift bag and created a matching card using a rubber stamp and assorted colors of handmade paper.

SQUASH AND WILD RICE SOUP

- 1/4 cup butter or margarine
- 1 cup finely chopped onion
- 1/2 cup finely chopped celery
- 3 cloves garlic, minced
- 5 cans (14.5 ounces each) chicken broth
- 1/2 cup uncooked wild rice
- 4 cups sliced zucchini
- 4 cups sliced yellow squash
- 1/2 cup shredded carrot
- 1/2 cup uncooked white rice
- 3/4 teaspoon salt
- 1/2 teaspoon ground black pepper
- 3/4 teaspoon dried basil leaves
- 1/2 teaspoon dried oregano leaves

In a large Dutch oven, melt butter over medium heat. Add onion, celery, and garlic. Stirring frequently, cook about 3 minutes or until vegetables are tender. Add chicken broth and wild rice. Bring mixture to a boil. Reduce heat to medium-low. Cover and cook 30 minutes.

Stir in zucchini, yellow squash, carrot, white rice, salt, and pepper. Increase heat to high and bring mixture to a boil. Reduce heat to low. Cover and simmer 20 minutes or until rice is tender.

Stir in basil and oregano. Serve hot. Store in an airtight container in refrigerator.

Yield: about 12 1/2 cups soup (1 gift)

STAMPED GIFT SET

You will need a large gift bag, a clear acrylic container to hold soup, a 4 1/2" x 6" cream-colored blank card with envelope to match, cream-colored and assorted colors of handmade paper to coordinate with bag, 2 5/8"w wired ribbon, an approx. 2 1/2"h rubber stamp with turkey design, black ink pad, black felt-tip pen with fine point, and a craft glue stick.

1. For turkey designs on bag and card, use rubber stamp and ink pad to stamp 4 turkeys onto cream-colored handmade paper, leaving at least 2" between designs. Leaving an approx. 1/2" border around each turkey, carefully tear designs from paper.

2. For bag, glue 3 stamped turkey designs to desired colors of handmade paper. Tearing 1/8" to 1/2" from edges of cream-colored paper, tear designs from colored paper. Glue designs to bag.

3. Line bag with a large sheet of colored handmade paper.

4. For card, tear an approx. 4 1/4" x 5 3/4" piece from desired color of handmade paper. Glue remaining stamped turkey design to center of colored paper piece about 3/4" from 1 short edge (bottom). Curving words slightly, use black pen to write "happy thanksgiving" on a piece of cream-colored handmade paper; tear greeting from paper. Glue greeting above turkey design on colored paper. Glue decorated paper to front of card.

5. For soup container, tear a square of colored handmade paper large enough to fit over lid. Center paper on lid and press edges down to sides of container. Tie ribbon into a bow around paper and container; trim ribbon ends. Stamp 1 turkey design at center of paper on lid.

FALL FLAVORS

*T*his fall, share Cranberry Mustard and Spicy Onion Chutney with friends who relish gourmet tastes. An embellished bag makes a nice keepsake.

CRANBERRY MUSTARD

- 2/3 cup finely chopped onion
- 2 tablespoons vegetable oil
- 6 tablespoons firmly packed brown sugar
- 2 teaspoons grated orange zest
- 2 cans (16 ounces each) whole berry cranberry sauce
- 2/3 cup prepared mustard

In a large skillet over medium heat, sauté onion in oil about 5 minutes or until onion is tender. Add brown sugar and orange zest. Stirring frequently, cook about 1 minute or until sugar dissolves. Add cranberry sauce and mustard; stir until well blended. Remove from heat and cool. Serve at room temperature as a condiment or use as a sauce for grilling. Store in an airtight container in refrigerator.

Yield: about 4 1/2 cups cranberry mustard (4 gifts)

SPICY ONION CHUTNEY

- 1/3 cup unsalted butter or margarine
- 1 cup firmly packed brown sugar
- 6 cups chopped onions (about 3 pounds onions)
- 3 cloves garlic, minced
- 1/2 cup orange juice
- 1/4 cup apple cider vinegar
- 2 tablespoons grated orange zest
- 6 whole cloves

Melt butter in a heavy Dutch oven over medium heat. Add brown sugar; stirring constantly until sugar dissolves. Cook 2 to 3 minutes or until sugar begins to caramelize. Add onions and garlic (sugar may harden a little); stirring constantly, cook about 10 minutes or until onions are tender. Stir in orange juice, vinegar, orange zest, and cloves; cook about 20 minutes or until mixture thickens. Remove from heat. Serve warm as a condiment with meat, breads, or vegetables. Store in an airtight container in refrigerator.

Yield: about 3 cups (3 gifts)

AUTUMN DAYS BAG

For each bag, you will need a brown gift bag, 2 coordinating fabrics to cover and line bag, paper-backed fusible web, 2/3 yd lengths of assorted ribbons to coordinate with fabrics, and a hot glue gun and glue sticks.

1. Follow manufacturer's instructions to fuse web to wrong side of fabric to cover bag. Cut a piece of fabric slightly smaller than front of bag; remove paper backing. Fuse fabric to bag.
2. Tie ribbon lengths together into a bow; trim ends. Glue bow to bag.
3. Line bag with remaining fabric.

CANDY CANE COOKIES

*W*ith their wintry
mint taste, Peppermint Candy
Cane Cookies really shine,
especially when presented in
star-studded cellophane bags!
The unique sacks showcase
your Yuletide spirit with style.

PEPPERMINT CANDY CANE COOKIES

$^1/_2$ cup butter or margarine, softened
$1^1/_4$ cups sugar
  1   egg
$^1/_2$ teaspoon peppermint extract
$2^1/_2$ cups all-purpose flour, divided
  1   teaspoon baking powder
$^1/_4$ teaspoon salt
$^1/_4$ cup milk
$^1/_2$ teaspoon red liquid food coloring

Preheat oven to 350 degrees. In a large bowl, cream butter and sugar until fluffy. Add egg and peppermint extract; beat until smooth. In a medium bowl, combine 2 cups flour, baking powder, and salt. Alternately add dry ingredients and milk to creamed mixture; beat until a soft dough forms. Add remaining $^1/_2$ cup flour, using hands to knead until well blended. Divide dough in half; tint half red. Cover with plastic wrap to prevent drying. For each cookie, shape about 1 teaspoon red dough into a 5-inch-long roll. Repeat with about 1 teaspoon plain dough. Place rolls on an ungreased baking sheet. Holding 2 pieces of dough together at ends, twist dough tightly together and press ends together to seal. Shape each cookie to resemble a candy cane, leaving about a 1-inch space in curved part of cookie. Place cookies 1 inch apart. Bake 8 to 10 minutes or until lightly browned on bottoms. Cool cookies on baking sheet 1 minute; transfer to a wire rack to cool completely. Store in an airtight container.

Yield: about 4 dozen cookies (8 gifts)

STARRY CELLOPHANE BAG

For each bag, you will need a 5" x 12" flat cellophane gift bag, a 4" square of clear cellophane, 1 yd of 1³/₈"w wired clear vinyl ribbon with gold edging, cream-colored paper, gold paint pen, assorted sizes of gold self-adhesive stars, tracing paper, transparent tape, and a hot glue gun and glue sticks.

1. Cut ribbon in half. With wrong side of ribbon facing bag, center 1 ribbon length on back of bag with 1 end of ribbon even with top edge; glue end in place. Fold remaining ribbon end around bottom of bag and glue to front.
2. Place gift in bag.
3. For flap, fold top of bag 4" to front; tape to secure. Tie remaining ribbon into a bow; trim ends. Glue bow to flap, covering ribbon end.
4. For tag, trace star pattern onto tracing paper; cut out. Use pattern to cut star from cream-colored paper. Use small dots of glue at each point of star to glue cellophane square to 1 side (front) of star. Trim cellophane even with edges of star. Use paint pen to write "enjoy!" at center of star and draw wavy lines along edges of star. Glue tag to bag.
5. Adhere stars to bag, ribbon, tag, and bow.

YULETIDE TOFFEE

*W*hether your friends have been naughty or nice, send them merry Christmas greetings with bags of Toasted Almond Toffee! Coated with rich chocolate and chopped nuts, the buttery chunks are nestled in fabric sacks that are embellished with greenery and your choice of Santa's famous list, the jolly old elf, or a simple gift tag.

Toasted Almond Toffee

2¼ cups slivered almonds, coarsely chopped, toasted, and divided
1 cup butter
1 cup sugar
⅓ cup water
1 tablespoon light corn syrup
½ teaspoon vanilla extract
1 cup semisweet chocolate mini chips, divided

Line 2 baking sheets with aluminum foil; grease foil. Butter sides of a very heavy large saucepan. Combine butter, sugar, water, and corn syrup in saucepan. Stirring constantly, cook over medium-low heat until sugar dissolves. Using a pastry brush dipped in hot water, wash down any sugar crystals on sides of pan. Attach a candy thermometer to pan, making sure thermometer does not touch bottom of pan. Increase heat to medium and bring to a boil. Cook, without stirring, until mixture reaches hard-crack stage (approximately 300 to 310 degrees). Test about ½ teaspoon mixture in ice water. Mixture will form brittle threads in ice water and will remain brittle when removed from the water. Remove from heat and stir in 1 cup almonds and vanilla. Spread mixture onto 1 prepared baking sheet. Sprinkle ½ cup chocolate chips over hot toffee; spread melted chocolate. Sprinkle ½ cup almonds over chocolate. Invert toffee onto second baking sheet. Sprinkle second side with remaining ½ cup chocolate chips; spread melted chocolate. Sprinkle remaining almonds over chocolate; press into chocolate. Chill 1 hour or until chocolate hardens. Break into small pieces. Store in an airtight container in a cool place.

Yield: about 1½ pounds toffee
(3 large or 4 small gifts)

Santa's Sacks

For each sack, you will need heavy cardboard, cream-colored paper, jute twine, silk greenery sprigs, thread to match fabric, Design Master® Glossy Wood Tone spray, brown felt-tip pen with fine point, tracing paper, craft knife and a cutting mat or folded newspaper, and a hot glue gun and glue sticks.
For each sack with Santa, you will *also* need a 6" x 12" fabric piece for sack, photocopy of Santa illustration (page 111), colored pencils, and spray adhesive.
For Santa's list sack, you will *also* need a 7½" x 22" fabric piece for sack, miniature gold pinecone, two 15mm red jingle bells, and red and black felt-tip pens with fine points.
For small sack, you will *also* need a 6¾" x 14" fabric piece for sack and a 15mm red jingle bell.

SACK WITH SANTA

1. Use colored pencils to color photocopy of Santa. Lightly spray Santa with wood tone spray. Cutting about ½" from Santa, cut out Santa. Use spray adhesive to glue Santa to cardboard. Use craft knife to cut Santa from cardboard.
2. For sack, follow Steps 2 - 5 of *Making a Sewn Fabric Bag*, page 122.
3. For sack bottom, trace small oval pattern, page 111, onto tracing paper; cut out. Use pattern to cut oval from cardboard. Place oval in bottom of sack.
4. For closure, cut a row of small slits about 1" from top of sack and about ¾" apart. Thread two 10" twine lengths through slits. Knot lengths together at each end; trim ends.
5. With bottom of Santa at bottom of sack, glue Santa to back of sack.
6. For tag, cut a tag shape from cream-colored paper. Use brown pen to write name and draw borders ⅛" from edges of tag. Lightly spray tag with wood tone spray.
7. Place gift in sack and tie twine to close sack.
8. Glue tag and greenery sprig to sack.

SANTA'S LIST SACK

1. For sack, follow Steps 2 - 5 of *Making a Sewn Fabric Bag*, page 122.
2. For sack bottom, trace large oval pattern, page 111, onto tracing paper; cut out. Use pattern to cut oval from cardboard. Place oval in bottom of sack.
3. Lightly spray bells with wood tone spray. Tie 1 bell onto each end of a 15" twine length.
4. Place gift in sack and tie twine into a bow around top of sack.
5. For list, cut an approx. 1½" x 6" strip of cream-colored paper. Use brown pen to write names on list. Use red and black pens to mark off or highlight names on list. Lightly spray list with wood tone spray. Wrap bottom of list around a pencil to curl.
6. Glue list, greenery sprigs, and pinecone to sack.

SMALL SACK

1. For sack, follow Steps 2 - 5 of *Making a Sewn Fabric Bag*, page 122.
2. For sack bottom, trace medium oval pattern, page 111, onto tracing paper; cut out. Use pattern to cut oval from cardboard. Place oval in bottom of sack.
3. Place gift in sack and tie a 15" twine length into a bow around top of sack; trim ends.
4. For tag, follow Step 6 of Sack With Santa instructions.
5. Lightly spray bell with wood tone spray. Glue tag, greenery sprigs, and bell to sack.

SOPHISTICATED CANDIES

F or tasteful Christmas gifts, present your friends and neighbors with rich Pecan-Chocolate Candies in elegant ribbon bags. The candies are delectable delights, and the opulent bags are made from lengths of wide wired ribbon. This gift is certain to be a palate-pleaser!

PECAN-CHOCOLATE CANDIES

- 1 package (12 ounces) butterscotch chips
- 1 package (10 ounces) peanut butter chips
- 1 package (6 ounces) semisweet chocolate chips
- 6 ounces chocolate candy coating
- 2 cups chopped pecans, toasted

Line a baking sheet with lightly greased waxed paper. Stirring constantly, melt butterscotch chips, peanut butter chips, chocolate chips, and candy coating in a heavy large saucepan over low heat. Stir in pecans. Drop candy by tablespoonfuls onto prepared baking sheet. Allow candies to harden. Store in an airtight container in a cool place.

Yield: about 70 candies (7 gifts)

RIBBON BAG

For each bag, you will need ¹/₂ yd of 5"w wired metallic ribbon, ³/₄ yd of 1¹/₄"w wired gold mesh ribbon, 1¹/₈ yds of gold braid, metallic thread to match 5"w ribbon, and a 1⁵/₈" dia. glass ball ornament.

1. To form bag, match wrong sides and ends and fold 5"w ribbon in half. Stitching close to wired edges, use metallic thread to hand sew side edges of ribbon together.

2. Place gift in bag.

3. Cut gold braid in half. Knot each end of each braid length. Tie gold ribbon and braid lengths together around top of bag. Thread 1 streamer of gold ribbon through hanger on ornament. Tie ribbon and braid into a bow; trim ribbon ends.

SPICY CHRISTMAS CIDER

*S*imple Spicy Christmas Drink Mix makes a deliciously fruity warmer when simmered with apple cider. And it's oh-so-easy to craft the unique gift bag! Just sponge paint a brown bag, glue on a "recycled" Christmas card, and tie it all together with gold ribbons.

SPICY CHRISTMAS DRINK MIX

- 4 cups water
- 1 cup sugar
- 5 cinnamon sticks
- 2 teaspoons whole cloves
- 2 cans (12 ounces each) frozen orange juice concentrate
- 2 cans (12 ounces each) frozen pineapple juice concentrate
- 1 can (12 ounces) frozen lemonade concentrate

Combine water and sugar in a large saucepan. Stirring constantly, cook over medium-high heat 4 minutes or until sugar dissolves. Reduce heat to low. Add cinnamon sticks and cloves; cover and cook 15 minutes. Strain mixture into a large heatproof container; discard cinnamon and cloves. Stir in orange, pineapple, and lemonade concentrates. Store in an airtight container in refrigerator. Give with serving instructions.

Yield: about 12 cups drink mix (6 gifts)

To serve: Heat $1/4$ cup drink mix with 6 ounces apple cider; serve hot. For a variation, add 1 tablespoon apple brandy to each serving of prepared hot drink.

CHRISTMAS CARD BAG

For each bag, you will need a brown lunch bag, an old Christmas card, 30" of $3/8$"w wired gold ribbon, red and metallic gold acrylic paint, small sponge pieces, newspaper, paper towels, $1/4$" hole punch, and a craft glue stick.

1. Use sponge pieces and follow *Sponge Painting*, page 121, to paint front of bag red, then gold.

2. Cut front from Christmas card. Center and glue card front to bag at least 3" from top.

3. Place gift in bag.

4. Fold top of bag about 1" to back; repeat.

5. Punch 1 hole in each side of folded part of bag. Cut ribbon in half. Thread 1 length of ribbon through each hole and tie into a bow; trim ends.

PEANUT BUTTER SNOWBALLS

*T o delight your child's
favorite schoolmates this
Christmas, send these
whimsical Peanut Butter
Snowballs. They're super easy
to make — just sandwich
peanut butter between vanilla
wafers, dip in candy coating,
and dust with sugar "snow."
Then pack the delicious
confections in our fabric-
covered gift bags. Decorated
with snowflake ornaments,
curling ribbon, and print
fabric motifs, the snowman
bags make cute carriers.*

PEANUT BUTTER SNOWBALLS

  1 cup creamy peanut butter
  1 package (11 ounces) vanilla wafers
 16 ounces vanilla candy coating
      White coarse decorating sugar

Spread about 1 teaspoon peanut butter on flat side of 1 cookie; top with second cookie. Repeat using remaining cookies and peanut butter. Melt candy coating in the top of a double boiler over simmering water. Remove from heat. (If candy coating begins to harden, return to heat.) Place each cookie sandwich on a fork and hold over pan; spoon candy coating over cookie. Transfer to waxed paper. Sprinkle cookies with sugar before coating hardens. Allow coating to harden. Store in an airtight container in a cool place.

Yield: about 3 dozen cookies (3 large or 6 small gifts)

FROSTY TREAT BAGS

For each bag, you will need snowman-motif fabric, paper-backed fusible web, and a 1/4" hole punch.
For appliqué bag, you will *also* need a small gift bag, coordinating curling ribbons, 16" of 11/4"w sheer white ribbon, and a pressing cloth.
For each fabric-covered bag, you will *also* need a medium-size gift bag; either 1 yd of 11/4"w wired sheer white ribbon, 6" of floral wire, and coordinating curling ribbons, or 14" of 21/2"w wired sheer white ribbon, 9" of 1/8"w satin ribbon, and a 4"w plastic snowflake ornament.

APPLIQUÉ BAG

1. Follow manufacturer's instructions to fuse web to wrong side of fabric. Cut desired snowman motif from fabric. Remove paper backing. Using a pressing cloth, fuse motif to front of bag.
2. Place gift in bag.
3. Fold top of bag about 1" to front. Punch 2 holes close together at center of folded part of bag.
4. Thread curling ribbons through holes and knot ribbons together at front of bag; curl ends. Tie sheer ribbon into a bow around knot of curling ribbons; trim ends.

FABRIC-COVERED BAG

1. Follow manufacturer's instructions to fuse web to wrong side of fabric. Cut a piece of fabric same size as front of bag. Remove paper backing; fuse fabric to front of bag.
2. Place gift in bag.
3. Fold top of bag about 11/2" to front or back. Punch 2 holes close together at center of folded part of bag.
4. For multi-loop bow with curling ribbon, follow *Making a Multi-Loop Bow,* page 123, to make a bow from 11/4"w ribbon. Thread 12/3 yd lengths of curling ribbon through holes in bag. Place bow on front of bag between holes. Tie curling ribbons into a bow over wired ribbon bow; curl ends.
5. For bow with ornament, thread 21/2"w ribbon through holes in bag. Tie ribbon into a bow at front of bag; trim ends. Thread ornament onto satin ribbon. Slip 1 end of ribbon behind knot of bow on bag and knot ribbon ends together; trim ends.

HO-HO-HOLIDAY LOAVES

If you're ho-ho-hoping for quick-and-easy Christmas gifts, stir up a batch of our yummy Peanut Butter-Banana Bread! Plain brown bags appliquéd with a cheery holiday message make for a festive delivery.

PEANUT BUTTER-BANANA BREAD

- 1/2 cup butter or margarine, softened
- 3/4 cup granulated sugar
- 1/4 cup firmly packed brown sugar
- 2 eggs
- 1 teaspoon vanilla extract
- 1 1/2 cups mashed bananas (about 3 bananas)
- 2 cups all-purpose flour
- 1 teaspoon baking powder
- 1/4 teaspoon salt
- 1 package (10 ounces) peanut butter chips

Preheat oven to 350 degrees. Grease four 3 1/4 x 6-inch loaf pans; line bottoms with waxed paper and grease waxed paper. In a large bowl, cream butter and sugars until fluffy. Add eggs and vanilla; beat until smooth. Add bananas; beat until well blended. In a medium bowl, combine flour, baking powder, and salt. Add dry ingredients to creamed mixture; stir just until moistened. Stir in peanut butter chips. Spread batter into prepared pans. Bake 45 to 50 minutes or until a toothpick inserted in center of bread comes out clean. Cool in pans 10 minutes. Remove from pans and cool completely on a wire rack.

Yield: 4 loaves bread

"HO-HO-HO" BAG

For each bag, you will need a brown lunch bag, fabrics for appliqués, paper-backed fusible web, 26" of heavy jute twine, and red tissue paper to line bag.

1. For appliqués, use patterns, page 111, and follow *Making Appliqués*, page 122, to make 3 of each letter. Remove paper backing.

2. Arrange letters on front of bag; fuse in place.

3. Line bag with tissue paper. Place gift in bag.

4. Knot each end of twine. Knot twine around top of bag.

WARMING WINTER COCOA

*A*fter a winter jaunt outside, what could be more warming than a cup of steaming Malted Cocoa? Surprise a snowbird friend with this chill-busting mix packaged in a jolly snowman bag that's easy and fun to make.

MALTED COCOA MIX

1 package (25.6 ounces) nonfat dry milk powder

6 cups miniature marshmallows

1 container (16 ounces) instant cocoa mix for milk

1 jar (13 ounces) malted milk powder

1 cup sifted confectioners sugar

1 jar (6 ounces) non-dairy powdered creamer

1/2 teaspoon salt

In a very large bowl, combine dry milk, marshmallows, cocoa mix, malted milk powder, confectioners sugar, creamer, and salt; stir until well blended. Store in an airtight container in a cool place. Give with serving instructions.

Yield: about 20 cups mix (10 gifts)

To serve: Pour 6 ounces hot water over 1/3 cup cocoa mix; stir until well blended.

SNOWMAN BAG

For each bag, you will need a white lunch bag, orange and black craft foam, two 3/4" dia. black buttons, a 2" dia. silk daisy, 41/2" of 7/8"w plaid ribbon, black felt-tip pen with broad point, tracing paper, and a hot glue gun and glue sticks.

1. Center a saucer upside down at top of flattened bag and draw around edge of saucer closest to opening of bag. Cut bag along drawn line. Fold top of bag about 31/2" to front.

2. For eyes, glue buttons about 1" apart near fold of bag.

3. Use black pen to draw irregularly shaped dots for mouth.

4. Trace nose and hat patterns, page 112, onto tracing paper; cut out. Use patterns to cut nose from orange and hat from black craft foam.

5. Glue ribbon to hat for hatband; trim ends even with edges of hat. Glue flower to hatband. Glue hat and nose to bag.

6. Place gift in bag. Glue edges of bag closed.

HOLIDAY HERBED PRETZELS

Soft home-baked pretzels make a great alternative for holiday snacking. Our flavorful recipe yields about five gifts — perfect for a fast, festive Yuletide fix! Package pretzel trios in holiday holly bags made by decorating white lunch sacks with fused-on silk leaves and painted "berries."

HERBED SOFT PRETZELS

- 1 cup milk
- 2 tablespoons fines herbes
- 2 tablespoons butter or margarine
- 1 package dry yeast
- 1 tablespoon sugar
- 1/2 cup warm water
- 4 to 4 1/2 cups all-purpose flour, divided
- 1 teaspoon salt
  Vegetable cooking spray
- 1 egg, lightly beaten
- 1 tablespoon water
- 4 teaspoons sesame seed
- 2 teaspoons coarse salt

In a small saucepan over medium heat, combine milk, fines herbes, and butter.

Heat just until butter melts; remove from heat and cool to lukewarm.

In a small bowl, dissolve yeast and sugar in warm water. In a large bowl, combine 4 cups flour and 1 teaspoon salt. Add milk mixture and yeast mixture to dry ingredients; stir until a soft dough forms. Turn dough onto a lightly floured surface. Knead about 5 minutes or until dough becomes smooth and elastic, using additional flour as necessary. Place in a large bowl sprayed with cooking spray, turning once to coat top of dough. Cover and let rise in a warm place (80 to 85 degrees) 1 hour or until doubled in size.

Turn dough onto a lightly floured surface and punch down. Separate into 16 equal pieces. Roll each piece into a 20-inch-long rope. Refer to Fig. 1 and shape each piece into a pretzel knot.

Fig. 1

Place 2 inches apart on a lightly greased baking sheet. Spray tops of pretzels with cooking spray; cover and let rise 20 minutes.

Preheat oven to 375 degrees. In a small bowl, combine egg and water. Brush pretzels with egg mixture and sprinkle with sesame seed and coarse salt. Bake 18 to 23 minutes or until golden brown. Transfer to a wire rack to cool. Store in an airtight container. Give with serving instructions.

Yield: 16 pretzels (5 gifts)

To serve: Place pretzels in a single layer on a baking sheet in a 375-degree oven. Heat 6 to 8 minutes or until warm.

CHRISTMAS HOLLY BAG

For each bag, you will need a white lunch bag, a silk holly pick, paper-backed fusible web, 16" of 1/8" dia. satin cord, iridescent red dimensional paint, red felt-tip pen with fine point, aluminum foil, 1/4" hole punch, and red tissue paper to line bag.

1. Remove leaves from holly pick, discarding any plastic or metal pieces. Use a warm, dry iron to press leaves flat.
2. Place a piece of foil shiny side up on ironing board. Place leaves wrong side up on foil. Lay a piece of web paper side up over leaves. Follow manufacturer's instructions to fuse web to leaves. Remove and save paper backing. Peel leaves from foil. Trim excess web from leaves.
3. Arrange leaves on front of flattened bag. Using saved paper backing as a pressing cloth, fuse leaves to bag.
4. For berries, paint red dots on bag.
5. For cuff, fold top of bag down about 1 1/4"; repeat. Use red pen to draw a dashed line to resemble stitching close to bottom of cuff.
6. Punch 2 holes close together at center front of cuff. Thread cord through holes and tie into a bow at front of bag; knot and fray ends.
7. Line bag with tissue paper.

CRANBERRY-NUT MINI CAKES

Scrumptious Cranberry-Nut Coffee Cakes bake up so effortlessly, you can make tasty Yuletide snacks for all of your co-workers — in one afternoon! Sponge-painted Christmas bags lined with red tissue paper make your gifts come alive with holiday cheer.

CRANBERRY-NUT COFFEE CAKES

TOPPING

2½	cups finely chopped fresh cranberries
2½	cups finely chopped pecans
¾	cup sugar
1¼	teaspoons ground cinnamon
¾	teaspoon ground allspice

CAKES

1	cup butter or margarine, softened
½	cup vegetable shortening
2½	cups sugar
4	eggs
1	tablespoon orange extract
1	tablespoon grated orange zest
3¼	cups all-purpose flour
1	teaspoon baking powder
¾	teaspoon baking soda
1	cup buttermilk

For topping, combine cranberries, pecans, sugar, cinnamon, and allspice in a medium bowl.

Preheat oven to 350 degrees. For cakes, grease a 6-mold fluted tube pan. In a large bowl, cream butter, shortening, and sugar until fluffy. Add eggs; beat until well blended. Stir in orange extract and orange zest. In a medium bowl, combine flour, baking powder, and baking soda. Add dry ingredients alternately with buttermilk to creamed mixture; beat until smooth. Sprinkle 1 tablespoon topping into each mold. Spoon 2 tablespoons batter over topping in each mold. Repeat with 1 tablespoon topping and 2 tablespoons batter in each mold. Bake 22 to 27 minutes or until a toothpick inserted in center of cake comes out clean. Cool in pan 5 minutes. Invert onto a wire rack and cool completely. Repeat with remaining topping and batter. Store in an airtight container.

Yield: about twenty-two 6-inch cakes (11 gifts)

SPONGE-PAINTED CHRISTMAS BAG

For each bag, you will need a brown lunch bag; Miracle Sponges™ (dry compressed sponges; available at craft stores); yellow, gold, red, light green, and dark green acrylic paint; yellow colored pencil; a 2" x 3¾" piece of kraft paper for tag; newspaper; paper towels; tracing paper; transparent tape (if needed); 18" of heavy-gauge floral wire; black felt-tip pen with fine point; and red tissue paper to line bag.

1. Trace tree and star patterns onto tracing paper; cut out.
2. Use patterns to cut shapes from dry sponges. Cut a ¾" x 2⅛" and a ¾" x 1¼" piece from dry sponge.
3. Use sponge shapes and paints and follow *Sponge Painting,* page 121, to paint designs on bag.
4. Use black pen to outline designs and draw swirls and small stars on bag.
5. Use yellow pencil to color small stars.
6. Line bag with tissue paper.
7. For tag, sponge paint 1 star near 1 short edge (left edge) of kraft paper piece. Use black pen to outline star, draw a border, write message, and decorate tag. Cut away left side of tag to reveal points of star. Curl about 2" of 1 end (top) of floral wire around a pencil. Use straight end of wire to pierce 2 holes in tag; move tag to top of wire just below curls. If necessary, tape tag to wire to secure. Place tag in bag.

53

FESTIVE RELISH

*F*or a gift anyone will
"relish," pack a garden-grown
gift of Sweet Zucchini and
Red Pepper Mix! To complete
the colorful delight, deliver
jars of the zesty condiment
in fabric-covered bags with
button closures.

SWEET ZUCCHINI AND RED PEPPER MIX

- 1 cup canning and pickling salt
- 2 quarts cold water
- 5 medium zucchini, cut in half lengthwise and cut into 1/4-inch slices
- 3 medium onions, cut into 1/4-inch slices and cut in half
- 3 sweet red peppers, cut into 2-inch-long strips
- 3 cups sugar
- 2 cups white vinegar
- 1 teaspoon celery seed
- 1 teaspoon mustard seed

In a large nonmetal bowl, stir salt into water. Place zucchini in salted water. Cover and let stand 2 hours.

Drain zucchini and thoroughly rinse with cold water. In a large bowl, combine zucchini, onions, and red pepper strips. In a large non-aluminum Dutch oven, combine sugar, vinegar, celery seed, and mustard seed. Bring vinegar mixture to a boil over high heat. Add vegetables; bring to a boil again and cook 3 minutes. Spoon mixture into heat-resistant jars; cover and cool. Store in refrigerator.

Yield: about five 12-ounce jars (5 gifts)

ENVELOPE-FLAP GIFT BAG

For each bag, you will need a brown lunch bag, a 4³/4" x 6¹/2" envelope, 2 coordinating fabrics to cover bag and envelope, paper-backed fusible web, 2 buttons, a 1³/4" x 3" piece of kraft paper for tag, 1 yd of cotton string, red and green felt-tip pens with fine points, ¹/8" hole punch, stapler, and a hot glue gun and glue sticks.

1. Follow manufacturer's instructions to fuse web to wrong sides of fabrics.
2. Cut a piece of 1 fabric about ¹/4" smaller on all sides than front of bag; remove paper backing. Center and fuse fabric to bag.
3. For flap on bag, draw around open envelope on paper side of remaining fabric; cut out shape. Remove paper backing. Fuse fabric shape to front and flap of envelope.

4. For point of flap on bag, fold each bottom corner of envelope diagonally to center back of envelope; glue to secure.
5. Place gift in bag. Fold top of bag about 1" to front; staple closed.
6. Moisten glue on envelope flap. With envelope flap at back of bag, place envelope over top of bag; press moistened flap to back of bag to secure.
7. Glue 1 button to flap about 1" from point. Glue remaining button to front of bag below point of flap.
8. For tag, use green pen to write message on kraft paper piece. Use red pen to draw dashed lines close to edges of tag to resemble stitching. Punch a hole in 1 corner of tag. Thread string through hole in tag. Loop string around buttons on bag and tie into a bow; trim ends.

ENTERTAINING CHEESE SPREAD

A French-inspired favorite, our Boursin Cheese Spread Mix makes a thoughtful gift for busy friends who like to entertain. They can create an instant appetizer by simply combining the mix with cream cheese! Present the mix in a penny sack, along with the serving instructions and a handmade card. A gift from St. Nick has never been more charming!

BOURSIN CHEESE SPREAD MIX

- 1 container (1⁵/₈ ounces) caraway seed
- 1 container (¹/₂ ounce) dried basil leaves
- 1 container (0.56 ounce) dried dill weed
- 1 container (0.12 ounce) dried chives
- ¹/₄ cup lemon pepper
- 2 tablespoons garlic salt
- 1¹/₂ tablespoons freshly ground black pepper

In a small bowl, combine caraway seed, basil leaves, dill weed, chives, lemon pepper, garlic salt, and black pepper. Store in an airtight container. Give with serving instructions.

Yield: about 2 cups dry mix (8 gifts)

To serve: For 2 cups cheese spread, combine 2 tablespoons mix with two 8-ounce packages softened cream cheese; beat until well blended. Serve with crackers.

CHEESE MIX GIFT CARD

For each gift card, you will need a penny sack, 1 photocopy each of Santa and label designs (page 113), red paper, a silk berry sprig, Design Master® Glossy Wood Tone spray, serrated-cut craft scissors, stapler, and a craft glue stick.

1. Lightly spray photocopies and red paper with wood tone spray.
2. Cut out Santa and label designs. Use craft scissors to cut an approx. 5" x 7¹/₂" rectangle from red paper for card.
3. Center and glue Santa design to card about ¹/₄" from 1 short edge (top). Center and glue label design to front of sack about ¹/₄" from bottom edge.
4. Place gift in sack. Fold top of sack about 1" to back.
5. Center sack on card so top of sack fits between Santa's hands. Place berry sprig on sack. Staple berry sprig and top of sack to card.

GOLDEN ANGEL CUPCAKES

*F*lavored with almond and poppy seed, Angel Cupcakes are heaven-sent! They're delightful snacks for anniversaries and a host of other occasions. The glittery gift bag and keepsake clothespin angel are inspirational studies in gift-giving ease!

ANGEL CUPCAKES

   1   package (16 ounces) angel food
        cake mix
   2   tablespoons poppy seed
1¹/₂ teaspoons almond extract, divided
 ¹/₂ cup chopped sliced almonds
1¹/₂ cups sifted confectioners sugar
   1   tablespoon plus 2 teaspoons water

Preheat oven to 350 degrees. Line a muffin pan with paper muffin cups. Prepare cake mix according to package directions, adding poppy seed and 1 teaspoon almond extract. Fill muffin cups about two-thirds full. Sprinkle batter with almonds. Bake 14 to 20 minutes or until tops are golden brown. Cool in pan on a wire rack. Transfer cupcakes to a wire rack with waxed paper underneath.

For icing, combine confectioners sugar, water, and remaining ¹/₂ teaspoon almond extract in a small bowl; stir until smooth. Drizzle icing over cupcakes. Allow icing to harden. Store in an airtight container.

Yield: about 2¹/₂ dozen cupcakes
(5 gifts)

CLOTHESPIN ANGEL BAG

For each bag, you will need a white lunch bag, a 4"h round wooden clothespin, 2¹/₂" of 2¹/₂"w white pregathered tiered lace, 15" of 1¹/₂"w wired gold ribbon, 7" of wired gold star garland, curly doll hair, gold glitter acrylic paint, iridescent gold dimensional paint, white spray paint, small sponge pieces, newspaper, paper towels, black felt-tip pen with fine point, and a hot glue gun and glue sticks.

1. Use sponge pieces and follow *Sponge Painting*, page 121, to sponge paint front of bag with gold glitter, then iridescent gold paint.

2. For angel, spray paint clothespin white. Use black pen to draw 2 dots for eyes on clothespin.

3. For dress, trim lace so gathered edge measures 1" and finished edge measures 2¹/₂". Glue gathered edge of dress to clothespin below head.

4. For wings, tie ribbon into a bow; trim ends. Glue bow to back of clothespin.

5. For hair, arrange and glue a small amount of doll hair to head.

6. For halo, coil star garland into an approx. 1" dia. circle; glue to head.

7. Place gift in bag. Fold top of bag about 1¹/₄" to front; repeat. Clip angel to top of bag.

OH BOY, GINGERBREAD!

As the rich aroma of fresh-baked gingerbread fills the air, friends will thank you for the thoughtful gift of Gingerbread Mix. Just write the recipe on a plastic bag, then fill it with the mix and deliver your offering in a gingham sack trimmed with a raffia bow and a cookie cutter. Nothing speaks more of country wholesomeness and simplicity!

GINGERBREAD MIX

7¹/₂ cups all-purpose flour

1¹/₄ cups granulated sugar

¹/₂ cup firmly packed brown sugar

3 tablespoons ground cinnamon

2 tablespoons baking powder

2 tablespoons finely chopped crystallized ginger

1 tablespoon ground ginger

1 tablespoon salt

2 teaspoons baking soda

2 teaspoons dried orange peel

1 teaspoon ground cloves

2 cups vegetable shortening

In a very large bowl, combine flour, sugars, cinnamon, baking powder, crystallized ginger, ground ginger, salt, baking soda, orange peel, and cloves. Using a pastry blender or 2 knives, cut in shortening until mixture resembles coarse meal. Store in an airtight container in a cool place. To give, follow Step 2 of Gingerbread Boy Bag instructions to decorate 4 plastic bags. Place about 3¹/₄ cups mix in each plastic bag.

Yield: about 13 cups gingerbread mix (4 gifts)

Gingerbread Cookie Instructions:
Make Your Own Gingerbread Boys!
1. Pour mix into large bowl.
2. Add ¹/₄ cup molasses, 2 tablespoons brewed coffee, and 1 lightly beaten egg; beat until well blended.
3. Roll out dough ¹/₈ inch thick on a floured surface. Cut out with cookie cutter.
4. Place 1 inch apart on an ungreased baking sheet; bake 6 to 8 minutes at 375°. Makes about 12 cookies.

GINGERBREAD BOY BAG

For each bag, you will need an 11" x 25" fabric piece for bag, ¹/₂"w paper-backed fusible web tape, an approx. 3¹/₄" x 4³/₄" gingerbread boy cookie cutter, a 1-quart resealable plastic bag, red paper, tracing paper, natural raffia, black permanent felt-tip pens with fine and medium points, and a hot glue gun and glue sticks.

1. Follow Steps 2 - 4 of *Making a Fused Fabric Bag*, page 122, to make bag from fabric.
2. Place plastic bag over gingerbread boys pattern, page 112, so pattern is centered just below seal of bag. Use medium-point black pen to trace pattern onto bag and copy Gingerbread Cookie Instructions, this page, onto bag.
3. Place plastic bag of mix in fabric bag.
4. Tie several lengths of raffia into a bow around top of bag.
5. For tag, trace heart pattern, page 112, onto tracing paper; cut out. Use pattern to cut heart from red paper. Use medium-point black pen to draw along outer edges of heart. Use fine-point black pen to write "oh boy!" on heart. Glue heart to cookie cutter. Glue cookie cutter to bag.

ANNIVERSARY WINE

*O*ur Citrus Wine is
a zesty anniversary gift for
a dear couple. The spirited
four-ingredient beverage
can be given in a bottle bag
that's easily crafted from
a wallpaper scrap. The fruity
drink also makes a delicious
cooler when mixed with
lemon-lime soda.

CITRUS WINE

  1 can (6 ounces) frozen orange
      juice concentrate, thawed
  1 can (6 ounces) frozen lemonade
      concentrate, thawed
  2 bottles (750 ml each) dry white
      wine
  1 cup orange-flavored liqueur

In a large container, combine juice
concentrates; strain and discard pulp. Stir
in wine and liqueur. Pour wine mixture
into bottles with lids. Store in refrigerator.
Serve chilled.

Yield: about 9 cups wine (3 gifts)

WALLPAPER BOTTLE BAG

For each bag, you will need a 9" x 27¼"
piece of wallpaper, a 2⅛" x 3⅛" piece of
cream-colored paper and two 2⅜" x 3⅜"
pieces of yellow paper for tag, 1¼ yds of
1½"w wired ribbon, tissue paper to line
bag, clear cellophane, a small silk leaf,
light brown colored pencil, black felt-tip
pen with fine point, tracing paper, a ¼"
hole punch, craft glue stick, and a hot
glue gun and glue sticks.

1. Fold short edges of wallpaper piece
1¼" to wrong side; use glue stick to
secure.
2. Fold long edges of wallpaper piece
1½" to wrong side. Matching wrong sides
and short edges, fold wallpaper piece in
half. Unfold last fold (bottom of bag).
3. Using glue stick, apply a line of glue
along each long edge on right side of
wallpaper piece. Refold bag and press
glued edges together.
4. For handle, cut a 14" length of ribbon.
Punch a hole about ½" below center top
of bag front and back. Thread ends of
ribbon length through holes to inside of
bag; knot ribbon ends. Hot glue ribbon
ends to inside of bag.

5. Tie remaining ribbon into a bow; trim
ends. Hot glue bow to front of bag at
bottom of handle.
6. For tag, trace lemon pattern onto
tracing paper; cut out. Use pattern to cut
lemon from 1 piece of yellow paper. Use
black pen to write "Citrus Wine" on
lemon. Use light brown pencil to draw
small dots on lemon. Use glue stick to
glue cream paper piece to center of
remaining yellow paper piece. Hot glue
leaf to back of lemon; glue lemon to
center of tag. Hot glue tag to bag.
7. Line bag with tissue paper. Wrap wine
bottle with cellophane. Place bottle
in bag.

58

MARMALADE MADE EASY!

*N*othing is more sweetly refreshing than delicious Orange Marmalade spread on an English muffin, a biscuit, or toast. Made with only three ingredients, our recipe couldn't be easier — and the gift sack is a cinch, too! Simply attach a colored tag made with a photocopied design and adorn the bag with a felt flower that blooms with springtime style!

ORANGE MARMALADE

- 7 unpeeled Valencia oranges
- 6 cups water
- 8 cups sugar

Thinly slice oranges crosswise; remove seeds. Cut orange slices into quarters. Place oranges and water in an 8-quart stockpot; bring to a boil over medium-high heat. Reduce heat to medium-low and simmer uncovered 1¹⁄₂ hours or until orange peel is translucent and tender. Add sugar; stir until sugar dissolves. Attach a candy thermometer to pan, making sure thermometer does not touch bottom of pan. Increase heat to high; boil rapidly until marmalade reaches 221 degrees or until a small amount of marmalade falls in 1 sheet when dropped from the side of a clean, dry metal spoon. (See *Testing Jelly*, page 123.) Remove from heat. Allow marmalade to cool 10 minutes. Spoon marmalade into heat-resistant jars with lids. Store in refrigerator.

Yield: about 9 half-pints marmalade (9 gifts)

SPRINGTIME FLOWERS BAG

For each bag, you will need a white lunch bag, assorted colors of felt, thread to coordinate with felt, ⁵⁄₈" dia. button, spring-type clothespin, photocopy of tag design (page 123), colored pencils, colored paper for tag background, desired color felt-tip pen, tracing paper, craft glue stick, and a hot glue gun and glue sticks.

1. For flower clip, trace flower, flower center, and leaf patterns, page 112, onto tracing paper; cut out. Use patterns to cut 1 flower, 1 flower center, and 2 leaves from felt.

2. Place flower center on flower; stitching through both layers, sew button to flower center. Hot glue leaves to back of flower. Hot glue flower to clothespin.

3. Place gift in bag. Fold top of bag about 1¹⁄₂" to front; repeat. Clip flower to top of bag.

4. For tag, use colored pencils to color photocopy. Use felt-tip pen to write names on tag. Cut out tag. Use glue stick to glue tag to colored paper. Cutting close to tag, cut tag from paper. Use glue stick to glue tag to bag.

CARAMELIZED PECANS

*F*elt flowers blossom on these pretty gift sacks filled with crunchy Caramelized Pecans, sugar-coated nuggets with a rich, delicious taste. To ensure that fond memories of your token will linger long after the snacks are gone, our colorful sack clips double as handy magnets to dress up a message center.

CARAMELIZED PECANS

Recipe does not work well if doubled.

　　　Vegetable cooking spray
　³/₄　cup sugar
　　2　tablespoons water
　　1　teaspoon vanilla extract
　¹/₄　teaspoon cream of tartar
　　2　cups pecan halves

Spray a sheet of aluminum foil and 2 forks with cooking spray. Combine sugar, water, vanilla, and cream of tartar in a heavy medium skillet over medium-low heat; stirring frequently, cook 10 minutes. Using a pastry brush dipped in hot water, wash down any sugar crystals on sides of pan. Stir in pecans. Increase heat to medium. Stirring occasionally, cook 10 minutes or until sugar begins to caramelize. Stirring constantly, cook 1 to 2 minutes until sugar is caramelized and pecans are golden brown (watch very closely to prevent burning). Spread on aluminum foil. Use forks to separate pecans; allow to cool. Store in an airtight container.

Yield: about 2¹/₂ cups caramelized pecans (2 gifts)

FELT FLOWER MAGNET BAG

For each bag, you will need a penny sack, assorted colors of felt, embroidery floss to coordinate with felt, ⁵/₈" dia. button, spring-type clothespin, 2" of self-adhesive magnetic tape, tracing paper, and a hot glue gun and glue sticks.

1. Trace flower, flower center, and leaf patterns, page 113, onto tracing paper; cut out. Use patterns to cut 1 flower, 1 flower center, and 1 of each leaf from felt.
2. Place leaves on a contrasting color of felt. Use embroidery floss to sew a running stitch along center of each leaf. Cutting close to leaves, cut leaves from felt.
3. Place flower center on flower; stitching through both layers, use embroidery floss to sew button to flower center. Glue leaves to back of flower. Glue flower to clothespin. Adhere magnet to opposite side of clothespin.
4. Place gift in sack.
5. Fold top of sack about 1" to back; repeat. Clip flower to top of sack.

HERBED HONEYS

Herbed Honeys make thoughtful gifts for gourmet cooks — or anyone who loves nature's choice sweetener! To create the delicate nectars, simply pour warm honey over your choice of herbs and allow the flavors to blend. For giving, nestle the jars in charming fabric-covered bags along with pretty flowers and wooden honey dippers!

HERBED HONEYS

4 cups honey
  Fresh herbs, washed and patted dry
    (we used sprigs of tarragon,
    thyme, and rosemary, and basil,
    mint, sage, and lavender leaves

Place honey in a medium saucepan over medium heat until warm. For each jar, bruise 2 sprigs or leaves of desired herb and place in a 4-ounce heat-resistant jar. Pour ½ cup warm honey over herb. Cover and let sit at room temperature 2 days. Replace bruised leaves with fresh herbs before giving. Use honey to sweeten tea, season meats, sweeten salad dressings, or serve with bread. Store at room temperature up to 3 weeks.

Yield: eight 4-ounce jars herbed honeys (4 large or 8 small gifts)

HONEY JARS AND BAGS

For each jar, you will need muslin, lightweight cardboard, polyester bonded batting (optional), brown felt-tip pen with fine point, and craft glue.
For each bag, you will need either a brown penny sack or lunch bag, fabric,

paper-backed fusible web, natural excelsior, and a black felt-tip pen with medium point.

1. For lid of jar, follow *Jar Lid Finishing*, page 122. Use brown pen to write recipe name at center of jar lid insert.
2. For bag, follow manufacturer's instructions to fuse web to wrong side of fabric.
3. Cut a piece of fabric same size or slightly smaller than front of bag; remove paper backing. Fuse fabric to front of bag.
4. For cuff, fold top edge of bag down about 1"; repeat. Use black pen to draw a dashed line close to bottom edge of cuff to resemble stitching.
5. Fill bag with excelsior.

BEER CHEESE PARTY PACKS

*S*erve savory Beer
Cheese Spread at your next
game-watching get-together,
then treat guests to take-
home party packs filled with
more of the tangy spread and
hearty crackers. Cute "cheese"
tags accent the colorful gift
bags, which are fast to finish
by gluing beer bottle labels
to plain lunch sacks.

BEER CHEESE SPREAD

> 4 cups (16 ounces) shredded sharp
>   Cheddar cheese
> 4 cups (16 ounces) shredded mild
>   Cheddar cheese
> 1 teaspoon dry mustard
> 1 clove garlic, minced
> $1/8$ teaspoon ground red pepper
> 1 bottle (12 ounces) beer
>   Crackers to give with gifts

Combine cheeses, dry mustard, garlic,
and red pepper in a large food processor;
process just until blended. Gradually add
beer through tube feeder; process until
well blended. Spoon mixture into four
12-ounce mugs. Cover and store in
refrigerator. Give with crackers.

Yield: about 6 cups cheese spread
(4 gifts)

62

BEER LABEL BAG

For each bag, you will need a brown
lunch bag, labels removed from beer
bottles, yellow paper, 22" of jute twine,
red felt-tip pen with fine point, tracing
paper, $1/4$" hole punch, and spray
adhesive.

1. Use spray adhesive to glue labels to
front of bag as desired.
2. For cuff, fold top of bag down
about $1^3/4$".

3. For tag, trace pattern onto tracing
paper; cut out. Use pattern to cut shape
from yellow paper. Use red pen to write
"Beer Cheese" on tag. Punch holes in tag
so that it resembles a wedge of cheese.
4. Punch a hole in cuff at front of bag.
Thread twine through hole in bag and 1
hole in tag and tie into a bow.

WARM COUNTRY THANKS

*S*ay *"Thanks!" with this easy-to-make country bag filled with classic Chocolate-Raisin-Oatmeal Cookies. We've given an old-fashioned favorite an updated flavor with chewy chocolate-covered raisins.*

CHOCOLATE-RAISIN-OATMEAL COOKIES

1¼ cups butter or margarine, softened
¾ cup firmly packed brown sugar
½ cup granulated sugar
1 egg
1 teaspoon vanilla extract
1½ cups all-purpose flour
1 teaspoon baking soda
1 teaspoon salt
1 teaspoon ground cinnamon
3 cups old-fashioned oats
1 package (7 ounces) chocolate-covered raisins

Preheat oven to 375 degrees. In a large bowl, cream butter and sugars until fluffy. Add egg and vanilla; beat until smooth. In a medium bowl, combine flour, baking soda, salt, and cinnamon. Add dry ingredients to creamed mixture; stir until a soft dough forms. Stir in oats and raisins. Drop by tablespoonfuls 2 inches apart onto a greased baking sheet. Bake 10 to 12 minutes or until edges begin to brown. Transfer to a wire rack to cool. Store in an airtight container.

Yield: about 5 dozen cookies (2 gifts)

"THANK YOU" BAG

For each bag, you will need a medium-size gift bag, fabrics for appliqués and tag, torn fabric square to line bag, paper-backed fusible web, poster board, kraft paper and black felt-tip pen with fine point for tag, and a hot glue gun and glue sticks.

1. For appliqués, use patterns, page 114, and follow *Making Appliqués,* page 122, to make letters to spell "THANK YOU,"

2 flowers, 2 flower centers, and 4 leaves from fabrics. Remove paper backing.
2. Fuse letters to bag. For flowers, arrange remaining appliqués on poster board; fuse in place. Cut flowers from poster board. Glue flowers to bag.
3. For tag, use kraft paper for tag center and follow *Making a Fabric-Backed Tag,* page 123. Use black pen to personalize tag. Glue tag to bag.
4. Line bag with torn fabric square.

I t only takes a twinkling to put together this divine thank-you tote! Just embellish a purchased gift bag with ribbon, eyelet trim, and a hand-colored angel of gratitude. To complete your token, include individually wrapped pieces of Strawberry Divinity, a heavenly confection made with simple ingredients. What a wonderful way to say, "You're an angel!"

STRAWBERRY DIVINITY

2   egg whites
1   package (3 ounces) strawberry
     gelatin
3   cups sugar
3/4 cup hot water
3/4 cup light corn syrup

Line a 9-inch square baking pan with aluminum foil, extending foil over 2 sides of pan; grease foil. In a large bowl, use a heavy-duty mixer to beat egg whites until stiff. Gradually beat in gelatin until well blended; set aside. Butter sides of a heavy medium saucepan. Combine sugar, water, and corn syrup in saucepan. Stirring constantly, cook over medium-low heat until sugar dissolves. Using a pastry brush dipped in hot water, wash down any sugar crystals on sides of pan. Attach a candy thermometer to pan, making sure thermometer does not touch bottom of pan. Increase heat to medium and bring to a boil. Cook, without stirring, just until mixture reaches hard-ball stage (approximately 254 degrees). Test about 1/2 teaspoon mixture in ice water. Mixture will roll into a hard ball in ice water and will remain hard when removed from the water. While beating at high speed, slowly pour hot mixture over egg whites; beat until candy thickens and begins to hold its shape. Spread into prepared pan; cool completely. Cut into 1-inch squares. Wrap candies individually in waxed paper. Store in an airtight container in refrigerator.

Yield: about 6 dozen pieces divinity (2 gifts)

ANGEL BAG

For each bag, you will need a medium-size gift bag, white paper, pregathered eyelet trim with beading, satin ribbon to fit in beading of trim, colored pencils, black felt-tip pen with fine point, craft glue stick, a hot glue gun and glue sticks, and tissue paper to line bag.

1. Trace pattern, page 115, onto white paper.
2. Use colored pencils to color design. Use black pen to draw over all traced lines except outline of heart and draw dashed lines just inside edges of heart to resemble stitching. Cut out heart.
3. Use glue stick to glue heart to bag.
4. Tie a 9" length of ribbon into a bow; trim ends. Hot glue bow to heart.
5. Measure around top edge of bag; add 1/2". Cut 1 length each of eyelet trim and ribbon the determined length. Thread ribbon through beading of trim. With straight edge of trim close to top edge of bag, hot glue trim around bag, overlapping ends at back.
6. Line bag with tissue paper.

TEACHER'S APPLE LOAF

Show your child's favorite teacher some well-earned appreciation with a yummy Caramel-Apple Loaf tucked in our letter-perfect gift bag!

CARAMEL-APPLE LOAVES

    1 package (18.25 ounces) spice
        cake mix, divided
    1 cup quick-cooking oats
    3/4 cup firmly packed brown sugar
    1/2 cup chopped pecans
    1/4 cup butter or margarine, softened
    1 1/4 cups applesauce
    3 eggs
    1 cup chopped dried apples
    3 tablespoons caramel ice cream
        topping

Preheat oven to 350 degrees. Grease three 4 x 8-inch loaf pans and line with waxed paper; grease waxed paper. In a medium bowl, combine 2/3 cup dry cake mix, oats, brown sugar, and pecans. Using a pastry blender or 2 knives, cut in butter until mixture is crumbly. In another medium bowl, beat applesauce and eggs until well blended. Add dried apples and remaining cake mix to applesauce mixture; stir just until blended. Spread 1 cup batter in each prepared pan. Sprinkle 1/2 cup oat mixture over batter in each pan. Repeat layers with remaining batter and oat mixture. Drizzle 1 tablespoon caramel topping over oat mixture in each pan. Bake 35 to 40 minutes or until a toothpick inserted in center of loaf comes out clean. Cool in pans 20 minutes. Remove from pans and cool completely on a wire rack. Store in an airtight container.

Yield: 3 loaves bread (3 gifts)

"CLASS-Y" TEACHER'S BAG

For each bag, you will need a 3"w wooden apple cutout with hole for hanger; a 9" x 26" fabric piece for bag; 1/2"w paper-backed fusible web tape; three 2/3 yd lengths of assorted satin ribbons for bow and a 2/3 yd length of narrow satin ribbon to fit through hole in apple cutout; red, green, and brown acrylic paint; paintbrushes; black felt-tip pen with medium point; and pinking shears.

1. For bag, follow Steps 2 and 4 of *Making a Fused Fabric Bag*, page 122.

Use pinking shears to trim top edge of bag.

2. For tag, use a pencil to draw outlines of leaves and stem on apple cutout. Paint apple red, leaves green, and stem brown. Use black pen to outline leaves and stem and to write "to a TEACHER with CLASS!" on apple.

3. Place gift in bag. Tie 3 ribbon lengths together into a bow around top of bag. Thread narrow ribbon length through hole in apple and tie into a bow around knot of bow on bag. Trim ribbon ends.

THANKS, TEACHER!

Two Crunchy Cheese Balls plus two chalkboard-inspired gift bags add up to fun "thank you" surprises for teachers. Sprinkled with spicy chili powder, the flavorful appetizers are prepared with a blend of cheeses and a secret ingredient for "crunch" — sauerkraut! Include crisp crackers in each of the bow-topped bags and instruct the teachers to enjoy!

CRUNCHY CHEESE BALLS

  2 packages (8 ounces each) cream cheese, softened
  2 cups (8 ounces) finely shredded sharp Cheddar cheese
  1 can (10 ounces) chopped sauerkraut, well drained
  1/4 cup finely chopped green onions
  2 teaspoons Worcestershire sauce
     Chili powder
     Crackers to give with cheese balls

In a large bowl, beat cream cheese until fluffy. Add Cheddar cheese; beat until well blended. Stir in sauerkraut, green onions, and Worcestershire sauce. Divide mixture in half; roll each half into a ball. Sprinkle each ball with chili powder. Wrap in plastic wrap; store in refrigerator. Give with crackers.

Yield: 2 cheese balls, about 2 cups each (2 gifts)

TEACHER'S GIFT BAG

For each bag, you will need a medium-size black gift bag, 1/2 yd of 1 1/2"w wired red and white gingham ribbon, white dimensional paint, white marking pencil, a new sharpened pencil for closing bag, 1/4" hole punch, and a hot glue gun and glue sticks.

1. Use white pencil to lightly write message on flattened bag; paint over letters with white paint.

2. Place gift in bag.
3. Fold top of bag about 2" to front.
4. Punch 2 holes about 1 1/2" apart in folded part of bag. Insert pencil through holes.
5. Tie ribbon into a bow; trim ends. Glue bow to bag.

*P*erk up a friend who's feeling under the weather with a hearty Garden Vegetable Casserole. Prepared with rice, cheeses, and fresh veggies, this vitamin-packed dish is especially cheering when delivered in our nifty casserole bag. The clever carrier is easily made using a mesh produce bag, kraft paper, and acrylic paints. Since this recipe makes two casseroles, you can take a warm one to your friend and freeze the other for a no-fuss dinner later.

GARDEN VEGETABLE CASSEROLES

1¹/₂	cups uncooked rice
5	large fresh tomatoes, peeled and sliced
3	small zucchini, sliced
3	small carrots, thinly sliced
2	medium green peppers, thinly sliced into rings
1	onion, thinly sliced and separated into rings
³/₄	cup water
6	tablespoons olive oil
6	tablespoons rice wine vinegar
3	tablespoons chopped fresh parsley
1	to 2 teaspoons hot pepper sauce
2	small cloves garlic, minced
1¹/₂	teaspoons salt
³/₄	teaspoon dried thyme leaves
³/₄	teaspoon ground black pepper
³/₄	teaspoon dried basil leaves
1¹/₂	cups (6 ounces) shredded mozzarella cheese
¹/₃	cup shredded Parmesan cheese

Preheat oven to 350 degrees. Grease two 7 x 11-inch baking dishes. Place ³/₄ cup of rice in each baking dish. Layer half of vegetables over rice in each dish. In a small bowl, combine water, oil, vinegar, parsley, pepper sauce, garlic, salt, thyme, black pepper, and basil; stir until well blended. Pour half of oil mixture over vegetables in each dish. Cover and bake 1 to 1¹/₂ hours or until vegetables are tender.

Uncover casseroles and sprinkle cheeses over vegetables. Bake uncovered about 10 minutes or until cheese melts. Serve warm.

Yield: 2 casseroles, 6 to 8 servings each

"EAT YOUR VEGGIES" MESH CASSEROLE BAG

For each bag, you will need a mesh produce bag large enough to accommodate a 7" x 11" baking dish (our bag measures about 10" x 21"); kraft paper; yellow, red, and green acrylic paint; small round and flat paintbrushes; 1¹/₄"h alphabet sponges (available at craft stores); ¹/₂ yd each of ³/₈"w yellow and ⁷/₈"w green grosgrain ribbon; black felt-tip pen with medium point; paper towels; a hot glue gun and glue sticks; and corrugated cardboard.

1. For label, measure width of bag; multiply by 2 and add 1". Cut a 4"w strip of kraft paper the determined length.
2. Use paints to paint an approx. ³/₄"w checked border design along long edges of paper strip. Use yellow paint and alphabet sponges and follow *Sponge Painting,* page 121, to paint the word "VEGGIES" at center of strip. Use black pen to write "eat your" next to "VEGGIES."
3. Overlapping ends about 1", glue ends of strip together. Centering words at front of bag, slip label over bag and glue at sides to secure.
4. Cut a piece of cardboard slightly larger than bottom of casserole dish. Place cardboard in bag. Place covered casserole dish on cardboard in bag. Knot ribbons together around top of bag; trim ends.
5. For tag, cut a 3" x 4" piece of kraft paper. Matching short edges, fold paper piece in half. Use paints to paint borders on front of tag to match borders on bag label. Use black pen to write "get well soon!" on tag. Glue tag to ribbon.

SPICY VANILLA-PEACH JAM

*W*hen your family reunion rolls around, why not award your loved ones a summertime treat — our *Spicy Vanilla-Peach Jam.* With only six ingredients, this spread is super easy to make. Everyone will think your gifts are just "peachy" when you nestle jars of the jam in stenciled bags!

SPICY VANILLA-PEACH JAM

 5 cups peeled, pitted, and coarsely
     chopped fresh peaches
 $1/4$ cup freshly squeezed lemon juice
 9 cups sugar
 $1^1/2$ teaspoons ground cinnamon
 2 vanilla beans (3 inches long each)
 1 pouch (3 ounces) liquid fruit
     pectin

Process peaches in a food processor until finely chopped. In a heavy large stockpot, combine peaches and lemon juice. Stir in sugar and cinnamon until well blended. Split vanilla beans and scrape seeds into peach mixture. Add vanilla beans. Stirring constantly, cook over low heat 4 minutes. Increase heat to high and bring mixture to a rolling boil. Stir in liquid pectin. Stirring constantly, bring to a rolling boil again and boil 1 minute. Remove from heat; skim off foam. Remove vanilla beans. Spoon jam into heat-resistant jars with lids. Store in refrigerator.

Yield: about 10 cups jam (10 gifts)

STENCILED MUSLIN BAG

For each bag, you will need a 6" x 18" piece of muslin; thread to match muslin; acetate for stencils (available at craft stores); yellow, red, and green acrylic paint; small stencil brushes; craft knife and cutting mat or folded newspaper; black permanent felt-tip pen with fine point; removable tape (optional); paper towels; a $1^3/4$" square of cream-colored paper and a 2" square of green paper for tag; jute twine; a $1/4$" hole punch; and a craft glue stick.

1. Referring to stencil cutting key and color key, page 116, follow *Stenciling,* page 122, to stencil peach at center of muslin about $4^1/2$" from 1 short edge (top edge of bag).
2. Follow Steps 2, 3, and 5 of *Making a Sewn Fabric Bag,* page 122, to make bag from stenciled muslin.
3. Fringe top edge of bag about $1/2$".
4. For tag, center and glue cream-colored paper to green paper. Use black pen to write the following on tag: Have a "Peachy" Day! Punch a hole in 1 corner of tag.
5. Place gift in bag. Form a multi-loop bow from $1^1/2$ yds of twine; knot a 12" length of twine around center of bow to secure. Thread 1 end of twine through hole in tag. Knot twine around top of bag.

PUMPKIN-PATCH FUDGE

*T*o delight a gardener who has a sweet tooth, try this scrumptious Creamy Pumpkin Fudge. Appealing to his or her love of nature will be a snap when you present the candy in a gift sack that bestows the promise of a bountiful pumpkin harvest!

CREAMY PUMPKIN FUDGE

1¹/₂ cups sugar
²/₃ cup evaporated milk
¹/₂ cup canned pumpkin
2 tablespoons butter or margarine
1¹/₂ teaspoons pumpkin pie spice
¹/₄ teaspoon salt
2 cups miniature marshmallows
1 package (12 ounces) vanilla baking chips
¹/₂ cup chopped walnuts, toasted
1 teaspoon vanilla extract

Line an 8-inch square baking pan with aluminum foil, extending foil over 2 sides of pan; grease foil. Butter sides of a heavy medium saucepan. Combine sugar, evaporated milk, pumpkin, butter, pumpkin pie spice, and salt in saucepan. Stirring constantly, bring mixture to a boil over medium heat; boil 12 minutes. Remove from heat. Add marshmallows, vanilla chips, walnuts, and vanilla; stir until marshmallows and chips melt. Pour into prepared pan. Chill until firm. Cut into 1-inch squares. Store in an airtight container in refrigerator.

Yield: about 4 dozen pieces fudge (4 gifts)

PUMPKIN SEED PACKET BAG

For each bag, you will need a small brown bag, a pumpkin seed packet, a 1⁵/₈" x 3³/₄" piece of green paper for tag, 1 yd of brown paper wire, green and dark green colored pencils, brown felt-tip pen with fine point, ¹/₄" hole punch, serrated-cut craft scissors, tracing paper, graphite transfer paper, masking tape, and a hot glue gun and glue sticks.

1. Use loops of masking tape to tape seed packet to center front of bag close to bottom edge.
2. Trace vine patterns, page 119, onto tracing paper. Use transfer paper to transfer vines to bag front at each side of seed packet. Use colored pencils to color vines.
3. Use craft scissors to trim top edge of bag. Place gift in bag. Fold top of bag to front and tuck under top edge of seed packet. Punch 2 holes close together at center of folded part of bag.
4. Thread paper wire through holes. For bow, form an approx. 2¹/₄"w bow loop in each half of paper wire. Wrap streamer of each loop around center to secure. Wrap end of each streamer around a pencil to curl.
5. For tag, use brown pen to write "creamy pumpkin fudge" on green paper piece. Glue tag to bag.

71

To: Cindy
From: Christy

A "bouquet" of *Sunflower Cookies is a cheery way to say "I'm thinking of you" to a friend. Present your gift in a stylish tote that's easy to make by fusing fabric to a white gift bag, gluing on some silk blossoms, and adding a bow. What a sunny surprise!*

SUNFLOWER COOKIES

- 1 cup butter or margarine, softened
- 1 cup sifted confectioners sugar
- 3/4 cup firmly packed brown sugar
- 1 egg
- 1 teaspoon vanilla extract
- 2 1/4 cups all-purpose flour
- 1/4 teaspoon salt
- 1/4 teaspoon yellow liquid food coloring
- 1 cup semisweet chocolate mini chips

In a large bowl, cream butter and sugars until fluffy. Add egg and vanilla; beat until smooth. In a medium bowl, combine flour and salt. Add dry ingredients to creamed mixture; stir until a soft dough forms. Tint dough yellow.

Shape about one third of dough into a 2-inch-diameter x 5-inch-long roll. Cover with plastic wrap and chill. Use a rolling pin to roll out remaining dough between 2 sheets of plastic wrap into a 14-inch wide x 8-inch-high rectangle. Use plastic wrap to transfer dough to a baking sheet and chill 1 hour.

Preheat oven to 375 degrees. Cut 1/8-inch slices from roll and place 3 inches apart on a lightly greased baking sheet. Place about 1 teaspoon chocolate chips on each slice of dough; lightly press into dough. For petals, make 1-inch-wide lengthwise cuts and 1/2-inch-wide crosswise cuts to form small rectangles in remaining dough. Cut each small rectangle diagonally to form 2 triangles (Fig. 1).

Fig. 1

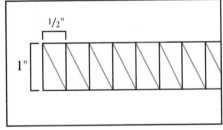

Press about 13 petals around each slice of dough to form a sunflower. (If dough becomes soft between batches, place in refrigerator.) Bake 4 to 6 minutes or until edges are lightly browned. Cool cookies on baking sheet 2 minutes; transfer to a wire rack to cool completely. Store in an airtight container.

Yield: about 2 dozen cookies (2 gifts)

SUNFLOWER BAG

For each bag, you will need a white gift bag with handles, solid black and black and white gingham fabrics for front of bag and tag, paper-backed fusible web, 1 1/4 yds of 1 1/4"w yellow craft ribbon, 3/4 yd of 1 3/8"w wired black and white gingham ribbon, 1/3 yd of 1/4"w black satin ribbon, 1/3 yd of 1/8"w black satin ribbon for tag, 3 small silk sunflowers and several leaves cut from stems, photocopy of tag pattern (page 123), white and black paper, floral wire, wire cutters, 1/4" hole punch, pressing cloth, and a hot glue gun and glue sticks.

1. Follow manufacturer's instructions to fuse web to wrong sides of fabrics and photocopy of tag.
2. Cut a piece of gingham fabric about 1" smaller on all sides than front of bag. Cut a piece of black fabric about 3/4" smaller on all sides than gingham fabric piece. Remove paper backing. Center and fuse fabric pieces to bag.
3. Arrange sunflowers and leaves on bag; glue to secure.
4. Follow *Making a Multi-Loop Bow,* page 123, to make 1 bow each from gingham ribbon and yellow ribbon. Place gingham bow on yellow bow. Knot 1/4"w black ribbon around centers of bows to secure. Use ends of 1/4"w ribbon to tie bows to handle of bag.
5. For tag, cut out photocopy of tag. Fuse a 2" x 3" piece of gingham fabric to white paper. Use pressing cloth to fuse tag to fabric-covered paper. Cutting about 1/4" from edges of tag, cut tag from fabric-covered paper. Glue tag to black paper. Cutting about 1/4" from edges of tag, cut tag from black paper. Punch a hole in 1 corner of tag. Thread 1/8"w black ribbon through hole and knot close to tag; tie tag to handle of bag.

CHOCOLATE BISCUIT MIX

*C*hocolate Biscuit Mix
will delight a cook. The lightly
sweet biscuits bake up with
lots of chocolaty chips and
crispy pecans. Present the mix
in a homespun fabric bag
along with a biscuit cutter
and the baking instructions.

CHOCOLATE BISCUIT MIX

1³/4 cups all-purpose flour
¹/4 cup cocoa
¹/4 cup sugar
1 tablespoon baking powder
¹/2 teaspoon salt
¹/4 teaspoon ground cinnamon
¹/2 cup butter or margarine
²/3 cup finely chopped pecans
¹/2 cup semisweet chocolate mini chips

In a large bowl, combine flour, cocoa, sugar, baking powder, salt, and cinnamon. Using a pastry blender or 2 knives, cut in butter until mixture resembles coarse meal. Stir in pecans and chocolate chips. Place about 2 cups mix in each of 2 resealable plastic bags. Store in refrigerator. Give with serving instructions.

Yield: about 4 cups mix (2 gifts)

To serve: Store mix in refrigerator until ready to serve. Preheat oven to 425 degrees. Place mix in a medium bowl. Add ¹/3 cup milk; stir just until a soft dough forms. On a lightly floured surface, use a floured rolling pin to roll out dough to ¹/2-inch thickness. Use a 2-inch-diameter biscuit cutter to cut out biscuits. Transfer to a greased baking sheet. Bake 10 to 15 minutes or until bottoms are lightly browned. Serve warm.

Yield: about 1 dozen biscuits

HOMESPUN BAG

For each bag, you will need an 8¹/2" x 26¹/2" fabric piece for bag, a 3¹/4" x 4¹/4" fabric piece for label, an approx. 1¹/2" x 30" torn fabric strip for tie, paper-backed fusible web, ¹/2"w paper-backed fusible web tape, photocopy of serving instructions (this page), kraft paper, 40" of jute twine, 2" dia. metal biscuit cutter, ¹/8" hole punch, pinking shears, brown felt-tip pen with medium point, and a craft glue stick.

1. For bag, follow Steps 2 and 4 of *Making a Fused Fabric Bag,* page 122. Use pinking shears to trim top edge of bag.
2. For label, follow manufacturer's instructions to fuse web to wrong side of fabric piece. Use brown pen to draw dashed lines about ¹/2" inside edges of fabric piece to resemble stitching and write "CHOCOLATE BISCUIT MIX." Trim edges of fabric piece with pinking shears. Remove paper backing; center and fuse label to bag about 2¹/4" from bottom.
3. Place gift in bag. Tie fabric strip into a bow around top of bag; trim ends.
4. For tag, cut out photocopied serving instructions. Glue instructions to kraft paper. Cut out tag close to edges of instructions. Punch a hole in tag. Thread jute through hole in tag and biscuit cutter. Tie jute into a bow around knot of fabric bow; trim ends.

A NEIGHBORLY WELCOME

A cordial welcome is the best way to make new neighbors feel right at home! And a gift of buttery chocolate Heart and Home Shortbread Cookies is sure to get your friendship off to a great start. Deliver the cookies in a simple fabric bag adorned with a house appliqué and a heartwarming gift tag.

HEART AND HOME SHORTBREAD COOKIES

    1   cup butter or margarine, softened
    1/2 cup sifted confectioners sugar
    1/2 cup firmly packed brown sugar
    1   teaspoon vanilla extract
    1   cup old-fashioned oats
    1/2 cup chopped pecans, toasted
    1 1/2 cups all-purpose flour
    2   tablespoons cocoa

In a large bowl, cream butter and sugars until fluffy. Beat in vanilla. Combine oats and pecans in a food processor; process until finely ground. In a small bowl, combine oat mixture, flour, and cocoa. Add dry ingredients to creamed mixture. Stir until a soft dough forms. Divide dough in half. Wrap in plastic wrap and chill 1 hour.

Preheat oven to 325 degrees. On a lightly floured surface, use a floured rolling pin to roll out dough to 1/4-inch thickness. Use a 2 3/4 x 2 3/4-inch house-shaped cookie cutter to cut out cookies. Transfer to an ungreased baking sheet. Use a 3/4-inch heart-shaped aspic cutter to cut out heart in center of each cookie. Bake 12 to 15 minutes or until bottoms

are lightly browned. Cool cookies on baking sheet 5 minutes; transfer to a wire rack to cool completely. Store in an airtight container.

Yield: about 3 dozen cookies (1 gift)

"WELCOME TO THE NEIGHBORHOOD" BAG

You will need a 15" x 30" fabric piece for bag, fabrics for appliqués and heart tag, paper-backed fusible web, thread to match bag fabric and fabric for door, 3/8" dia. gold shank button for doorknob, 3"w wooden heart cutout, miniature spring-type wooden clothespin, natural raffia, parchment paper, desired color felt-tip pen with fine point, and a hot glue gun and glue sticks.

1. For bag, follow *Making a Sewn Fabric Bag,* page 122.

2. For appliqués, use patterns, page 116, and follow *Making Appliqués,* page 122, to make 2 windows and 1 of each remaining shape. Remove paper backing.
3. Arrange appliqués on bag, overlapping roof, gable, and house appliqués about 1/8"; fuse in place.
4. For doorknob, sew button to door.
5. Place gift in bag. Tie raffia into a bow around top of bag; trim ends.
6. For heart tag, fuse web to wrong side of fabric. Draw around wooden heart on paper side of fabric. Cut heart from fabric about 1/8" inside drawn lines. Remove paper backing. Center and fuse fabric heart to wooden heart. Cut a 7/8" x 3" strip of parchment paper; notch ends. Use felt-tip pen to write "WELCOME" on paper strip. Glue paper strip to heart. Glue clothespin to back of heart. Clip heart to bow.

Everyone loves fresh homemade pizza, and with these Pepperoni-Veggie Pizza Kits, all the ingredients are included in one handy, taste-tempting gift! You can pack the dough mix, sauce, pepperoni, and mozzarella cheese in a simple basket. Then embellish the carrier with garlic and pepper picks for a presentation that's sure to please at "ciao" time!

PIZZA KITS

The Pizza Kits recipe makes 3 gifts; each gift makes two 12-inch pizzas.

PIZZA DOUGH MIX

- 11¼ cups all-purpose flour, divided
- 3 packages dry yeast, divided
- 3 teaspoons sugar, divided
- 1½ teaspoons salt, divided

PIZZA SAUCE

- 3 tablespoons olive oil
- 1 cup finely chopped onion
- 5 cloves garlic, minced
- 1 green pepper, chopped
- 1 can (29 ounces) tomato sauce
- 3 large ripe tomatoes, peeled and chopped (about 2 cups)
- 1 jar (6 ounces) sliced mushrooms, drained
- 1 can (6 ounces) tomato paste
- 2 cans (2¼ ounces each) sliced ripe olives, drained
- 2 tablespoons chopped fresh basil leaves
- 2 tablespoons chopped fresh oregano leaves
- ¾ teaspoon salt
- ½ teaspoon ground black pepper
- ½ teaspoon sugar
- ¼ teaspoon crushed red pepper flakes
- Three 8-ounce packages shredded mozzarella cheese and three 8.5-ounce packages pepperoni slices to give with gifts

For pizza dough mix, combine the following ingredients in each of 3 resealable plastic bags: 3¾ cups flour, 1 package yeast, 1 teaspoon sugar, and ½ teaspoon salt.

For pizza sauce, heat oil in a large Dutch oven over medium-low heat. Add onion, garlic, and green pepper. Stirring frequently, cook until vegetables are tender. Add tomato sauce, tomatoes, mushrooms, tomato paste, olives, basil, oregano, salt, black pepper, sugar, and red pepper flakes; simmer uncovered 20 minutes or until thickened. Remove from heat and cool. Place 2½ cups sauce in each of 3 containers. Cover and store sauce in refrigerator.

For each gift, give 1 bag Pizza Dough Mix, 1 container (2½ cups) Pizza Sauce, 1 package mozzarella cheese, 1 package pepperoni slices, and recipe for Pepperoni-Veggie Pizza (see Step 2 of Pizza Kit Basket instructions).

PEPPERONI-VEGGIE PIZZA

- 1 bag Pizza Dough Mix
- 1½ cups very warm water
- 2 tablespoons vegetable oil
- 1 container Pizza Sauce
- 1 package pepperoni slices
- 1 package shredded mozzarella cheese

In a large bowl, combine Pizza Dough Mix, very warm water, and oil; stir until a soft dough forms. Turn dough onto a lightly floured surface. Knead about 5 minutes or until dough becomes smooth and elastic, using additional flour as necessary. Cover and allow dough to rest 10 minutes. Divide dough in half and press into 2 lightly greased 12-inch pizza pans. Cover and let rise in a warm place (80 to 85 degrees) 30 minutes.

Preheat oven to 425 degrees. Bake crusts 10 minutes. Spread 1¼ cups Pizza Sauce over each partially baked crust. Place pepperoni slices on each pizza. Sprinkle 1 cup mozzarella cheese over each pizza. Bake 10 to 12 minutes or until crust is lightly browned and cheese is melted.

Yield: two 12-inch pizzas

PIZZA KIT BASKET

For each basket, you will need a large basket with handle, a red plaid kitchen towel, 2 brown lunch bags, two 9" lengths of 1½"w white and red check grosgrain ribbon, photocopy of recipe (page 117), 2 white 1½" x 2¾" self-adhesive labels, red felt-tip pen with medium point, red paper, artificial garlic and pepper picks, natural raffia, 12" of floral wire, stapler, and a craft glue stick.

1. Place Pizza Dough Mix and Pizza Sauce in bags. Fold top of each bag about 2" to front. Fold 1 length of ribbon over top of each bag; staple ribbon in place. Use red pen to write "Pizza Dough Mix" and "Pizza Sauce" on labels. Adhere labels to bags over ribbons.

2. For recipe card, cut out photocopy of recipe. Use glue stick to glue recipe to red paper. Cutting close to recipe, cut recipe from red paper.

3. Use floral wire to attach garlic and pepper picks to handle of basket. Tie several lengths of raffia into a bow over ends of picks; trim ends.

4. Line basket with towel. Place bags of dough mix and sauce, cheese, pepperoni, and recipe card in basket.

ALPHABET SCRAMBLE

*D*on't be puzzled about what to give someone who loves crossword puzzles! Our Alphabet Scramble snack mix — as easy as A-B-C to make — combines cereal, dried fruit bits, and honey-roasted almonds. For a presentation that spells fun, a brightly colored gift bag is decorated with a ribbon-tied puzzle book, sharpened pencils, and a thoughtful note.

ALPHABET SCRAMBLE

  10 cups sweetened alphabet-shaped cereal

   2 packages (6 ounces each) dried fruit bits

   2 cans (6 ounces each) honey-roasted whole almonds

Combine cereal, fruit bits, and almonds in a large bowl. Store in an airtight container.

Yield: about 16 cups snack mix (1 gift)

PUZZLE LOVER'S BAG

You will need a large gift bag, puzzle book, 1"w grosgrain ribbon, 2 sharpened pencils, a 2³/₄" square of white paper for tag, black ball-point pen, tissue paper to line bag, and a craft knife and small cutting mat or folded newspaper.

1. Center puzzle book on front of flattened bag. Use a pencil to draw an approx. 1¹/₄" line at center of top, bottom, and each side of book.

2. Place cutting mat inside front of bag. Use craft knife to cut a slit along each line.

3. To attach book to bag, measure height of puzzle book; multiply by 3. Cut a length of ribbon the determined measurement. From outside of bag, insert ribbon into slit at top of bag and out of slit at bottom of bag. Measure width of puzzle book; multiply by 3. Cut a length of ribbon the determined measurement. Insert ribbon through slits at sides of bag.

4. Center puzzle book on bag between ribbons. Knot ends of 1 ribbon length at center of book. Knot ends of remaining ribbon length at center of book. Trim ribbon ends.

5. Tuck pencils under ribbons.

6. For tag, use black pen to write message on paper piece. Tuck tag into top of puzzle book.

7. Line bag with tissue paper.

MOO-COW MOCHA

Those who enjoy country cow novelties will be charmed by these bags of Mocha Creamer! The mix stirs together quickly, and the bovine-inspired gift bags are simple to make by sponge painting plain white lunch sacks. This fast, friendly present will have everyone in the "moo-o-o-d" for mocha!

MOCHA CREAMER

  1 jar (6 ounces) non-dairy
       powdered creamer
  1 cup chocolate mix for milk
  1/2 teaspoon ground cinnamon

In a medium bowl, combine creamer, chocolate mix, and cinnamon. Store in an airtight container. Give with serving instructions.

Yield: about 2 1/2 cups creamer (4 gifts)

To serve: Stir 1 tablespoon creamer into 6 ounces of hot coffee.

COW-PRINT BAG

For each bag, you will need a white lunch bag, white and red paper for tag, 1/2 yd of 1 3/8"w wired red and white gingham ribbon, 10" of 1/8"w black satin ribbon, Miracle Sponges™ (dry compressed sponges; available at craft stores), black acrylic paint, black felt-tip pen with fine point, stapler, 1/8" hole punch, newspaper, paper towels, tracing paper, craft glue stick, and a hot glue gun and glue sticks.

1. Trace spot patterns onto tracing paper; cut out.
2. Use patterns to cut shapes from dry sponges.
3. Use sponge shapes and follow *Sponge Painting*, page 121, to paint black spots on bag.
4. Place gift in bag.
5. For flap, fold top corners of bag diagonally to center front. Fold point to front. Staple bag closed.

6. Tie wired ribbon into a bow; trim ends. Hot glue bow to bag.
7. For tag, cut a piece of white paper. Use black pen to write the following on tag: IN THE "MOO-O-O-D" FOR MOCHA COFFEE? Use glue stick to glue tag to red paper. Cutting close to tag, cut tag from red paper. Punch a hole in 1 corner of tag. Thread satin ribbon through hole and tie tag to bow on bag; trim ends.

Lovely lace-adorned bags filled with rich Hazelnut Coffee Fudge are just the way to say "I care."

HAZELNUT COFFEE FUDGE

- 3 cups sugar
- 1 cup strongly brewed hazelnut-flavored coffee
- 1 cup whipping cream
- 2 tablespoons butter
- 1/2 teaspoon cream of tartar
- 1/4 teaspoon salt
- 1 1/2 cups chopped hazelnuts, toasted
- 1/2 teaspoon ground cinnamon

Line an 8-inch square baking pan with aluminum foil, extending foil over 2 sides of pan; grease foil. Butter sides of a heavy Dutch oven. Combine sugar, coffee, whipping cream, butter, cream of tartar, and salt in Dutch oven. Stirring constantly, cook over medium-low heat until sugar dissolves. Using a pastry brush dipped in hot water, wash down any sugar crystals on sides of pan. Attach a candy thermometer to pan, making sure thermometer does not touch bottom of pan. Increase heat to medium and bring to a boil. Cook, without stirring, until mixture reaches approximately 236 degrees. Test about 1/2 teaspoon mixture in ice water. Mixture will easily form a ball in ice water but will flatten when held in your hand. Remove from heat; pour mixture into a large heatproof bowl. Place bowl in 2 inches of cold water in sink; do not stir. Cool to approximately 110 degrees. Remove from sink. Using high speed of an electric mixer, beat until fudge thickens and begins to lose its gloss. Stir in hazelnuts and cinnamon. Pour into prepared pan. Cool completely. Cut into 1-inch squares. Store in an airtight container in refrigerator.

Yield: about 4 1/2 dozen pieces fudge (3 large or 9 small gifts)

LACY BROWN BAGS

For each bag, you will need beige paper, gold paint pen with fine point, black felt-tip pen with fine point, serrated-cut craft scissors, tracing paper, and a hot glue gun and glue sticks.

For doily-trimmed bag, you will *also* need a brown lunch bag, a 7 1/2" dia. ecru doily, spray adhesive, and 2/3 yd of 7/8"w satin ribbon.

For fan-fold bag, you will *also* need a brown bottle bag, 1/2 yd of 4 7/8"w ecru flat lace, 2/3 yd of 7/8"w satin ribbon, and the following items for stickpin: a large darning needle, a 3/4"w heart charm, assorted beads, 1/4 yd of 1/8"w satin ribbon, small household sponge, and spray adhesive.

For small lace-covered bag, you will *also* need a penny sack, one 4" length and one 7" length of 2 1/2"w ecru lace, 1/2 yd of 1/8"w satin ribbon, and a large needle.

DOILY-TRIMMED BAG

1. Use spray adhesive to glue doily to back of bag with doily centered on bag and 1 edge of doily extending about 1" beyond top of bag. Fold top of bag about 4" to front.
2. For tag, trace heart pattern onto tracing paper; cut out. Use gold paint pen to draw around heart pattern on beige paper. Cutting close to heart, use craft scissors to cut out heart. Use black pen to personalize tag.
3. Tie ribbon into a bow; trim ends. Hot glue bow and tag to bag.

FAN-FOLD BAG

1. Use spray adhesive to glue lace to front of bag with lace centered on bag. Trim ends even with top and bottom of bag.
2. For stickpin, thread beads onto large end of needle; hot glue to secure. Tie 1/8"w ribbon into a bow around needle where 2 beads touch; trim ends. For bottom of stickpin, cut a thin piece of sponge slightly smaller than heart charm; hot glue sponge piece to back of charm.
3. For tag, follow Step 2 of Doily-Trimmed Bag instructions.
4. Place gift in bag.
5. Tie 7/8"w ribbon into a bow; trim ends. Fan fold top of bag. Insert stickpin through folds of bag, bow knot, and sponge backing on charm. Use a small dot of hot glue to glue tag to back of charm.

SMALL LACE-COVERED BAG

1. Use small dots of glue at edges of lace to glue 7" lace length along center front of bag. Trim ends even with top and bottom of bag. Glue 4" lace length to back of bag with 1 long edge extending about 1/2" beyond top of bag; trim ends even with sides of bag.
2. Cut a 10" length of ribbon. Thread ribbon onto needle. Beginning 2 1/2" from top of bag, weave ribbon through center of lace on front of bag. Unthread needle and glue about 1" at end of ribbon to bottom of bag. Thread remaining ribbon length onto needle. Beginning at bottom long edge of lace, weave ribbon through center of lace on back of bag. Unthread needle and glue about 1/2" at end of ribbon to back of bag.
3. Place gift in bag. Fold top of bag about 1" to front. Tie ribbons into a bow; trim ends.
4. For tag, follow Step 2 of Doily-Trimmed Bag instructions.
5. Glue tag to bag.

Nothing tastes better than fresh homemade bread! Our Sourdough Baguettes lend French charm to even the simplest meal. Present baked loaves in brown bottle bags decorated with raffia and photocopied tags and labels. You can also include a batch of the starter and the recipe so your friends can enjoy the baguettes anytime!

SOURDOUGH STARTER

     1 package dry yeast
$2^{1}/_{2}$ cups warm water, divided
     2 cups all-purpose flour
     3 tablespoons sugar
$^1/_2$ teaspoon salt

In a large nonmetal bowl, dissolve yeast in $^1/_2$ cup warm water. With a wooden spoon, combine remaining 2 cups warm water, flour, sugar, and salt. Loosely cover bowl or transfer starter into a $1^1/_2$-quart pitcher with lid, keeping spout open. Place container in a warm place (80 to 85 degrees) free of drafts 3 days. Stir mixture several times each day.

To use starter, remove amount needed for recipe. To replenish starter, stir in $^2/_3$ cup warm water and $^2/_3$ cup flour for each $^2/_3$ cup starter that is removed. Let stand at room temperature overnight and then store in refrigerator. Use and replenish starter every 7 to 10 days.

Yield: about 4 cups starter

SOURDOUGH BAGUETTES

$4^1/_2$ to 5 cups all-purpose flour, divided
     1 cup plus 2 tablespoons warm water
$^2/_3$ cup Sourdough Starter, at room
        temperature
$^3/_4$ teaspoon salt
        Vegetable cooking spray
     1 tablespoon yellow cornmeal
     1 egg white
     1 tablespoon water

In a large nonmetal bowl, use a wooden spoon to combine $2^1/_2$ cups flour, warm water, and starter. Cover mixture loosely with plastic wrap and let rest in a warm place (80 to 85 degrees) 5 hours or until doubled in size.

Stir in 2 cups flour and salt. Turn dough onto a lightly floured surface. Knead 5 minutes or until dough becomes smooth and elastic, adding additional flour as necessary. Place in a large bowl sprayed with cooking spray, turning once to coat top of dough. Cover loosely with plastic wrap and let rise in a warm place 12 hours or until doubled in size.

Turn dough onto a lightly floured surface and punch down. Knead dough 2 to 3 minutes; divide into thirds. Shape each piece of dough into a 12-inch-long loaf. Place loaves on a baking sheet that has been lightly greased with cooking spray and sprinkled with cornmeal. Spray loaves with cooking spray. Loosely cover loaves with plastic wrap and let rise in a warm place 4 hours or until doubled in size.

Preheat oven to 400 degrees. Use a sharp knife to make diagonal cuts across tops of loaves. In a small bowl, lightly beat egg white and water; brush on loaves. Bake about 20 to 25 minutes or until bread is golden brown and sounds hollow when tapped.

Serve warm or transfer to a wire rack to cool completely. Store in an airtight container.

Yield: 3 loaves bread

"HOMEMADE" BOTTLE BAG

For each bag, you will need a brown bottle bag, 1 photocopy each of label design (page 117) and tag design (page 123), black paper, natural raffia, Design Master® Glossy Wood Tone spray, black felt-tip pen with fine point, craft glue stick, and a hot glue gun and glue sticks.

1. Lightly spray photocopies with wood tone spray. Cut out label and tag.
2. Use glue stick to glue label to center front of bag.
3. Tie several raffia lengths into a bow; trim ends. Hot glue bow to bag.
4. For tag, use glue stick to glue tag to black paper. Cutting close to tag, cut tag from black paper. Use black pen to personalize tag. Hot glue tag to bow.

DRESS-UP PARTY POPCORN

*E*very little girl dreams of being a princess, so on her highness' next birthday, treat her and her guests to a wish come true! Our Peanut Butter Candied Corn will disappear like magic! Present the yummy popcorn in favor bags adorned with fun stickers and shimmering bows. Ponytail holders make pretty dress-up keepsakes.

PEANUT BUTTER CANDIED CORN

    4 quarts popped popcorn
    1 can (12 ounces) lightly salted
       peanuts
    1 cup firmly packed brown sugar
  3/4 cup dark corn syrup
  1/2 cup butter or margarine
  1/2 teaspoon salt
  3/4 cup smooth peanut butter
    1 teaspoon vanilla extract
  1/2 teaspoon baking soda

Preheat oven to 250 degrees. Combine popcorn and peanuts in a large roasting pan. In a large saucepan, combine brown sugar, corn syrup, butter, and salt over medium heat. Stirring constantly, bring to a boil; boil 1 minute. Remove from heat. Add peanut butter and vanilla; stir until smooth. Stir in baking soda (mixture will foam). Pour over popcorn mixture; stir until well coated. Bake 1 hour, stirring every 15 minutes. Spread on lightly greased aluminum foil to cool. Store in an airtight container.

Yield: about 20 cups candied corn (10 gifts)

PARTY FAVOR BAG

For each bag, you will need a white lunch bag, 1 sheet of stickers to fit on front of bag, 3/4 yd of 6"w pink tulle ribbon, a beaded ponytail holder to coordinate with ribbon and stickers, 1/4" hole punch, and transparent tape.

1. Leaving about 4" uncovered at top of bag, tape sticker sheet to front of bag.

2. Place gift in bag.
3. Fold top of bag about 1" to front; repeat.
4. Punch 2 holes about 1" apart at center of folded part of bag.
5. Thread ribbon through holes and tie into a bow over ponytail holder at front of bag; trim ends.

FUN FUNNEL CAKE MIX

F or a wonderful whiz of a gift, share our four-star Funnel Cake Mix! It's a breeze to prepare fluffy, sugar-dusted treats using the mix, which is delivered in a scarecrow bag. What a clever thought to top the bag with a funnel "hat!"

FUNNEL CAKE MIX

- 1¼ cups all-purpose flour
- 2 tablespoons nonfat dry milk powder
- 1 tablespoon sugar
- 1 teaspoon baking powder
- ⅛ teaspoon salt

In a medium bowl, combine flour, dry milk, sugar, baking powder, and salt. Store in an airtight container in a cool place. Give with serving instructions.

Yield: about 1½ cups mix (1 gift)

To serve: Heat about ½ inch vegetable oil in a large skillet over medium heat. In a medium bowl, combine mix, 1 cup lemon-lime soft drink, and 1 egg; beat until well blended. Cover end of funnel with finger. Hold funnel over skillet and pour about ¼ cup batter into funnel. Remove finger from funnel and, beginning in center of skillet, release batter in a circular motion toward outside of skillet. Using 2 spatulas to turn, fry funnel cake about 1 minute on each side or until golden brown. Drain cake on paper towels. Sprinkle with confectioners sugar. Repeat with remaining batter. Serve warm.

Yield: about 7 funnel cakes

SCARECROW BAG

You will need a brown lunch bag, fabrics for appliqués, paper-backed fusible web, two ⅝" dia. buttons, natural raffia, an approx. 4⅝" dia. metal funnel, 12" of floral wire, black felt-tip pen with fine point, and a hot glue gun and glue sticks.

1. For appliqués, use patterns and follow *Making Appliqués*, page 122, to make 1 nose and 2 cheeks from fabrics; remove paper backing.
2. Fuse nose to center front of flattened bag about 2" from bottom. Fuse cheeks to bag.

3. For mouth, use black pen to draw a curved, dashed line from cheek to cheek.
4. For eyes, glue buttons to bag.
5. Place gift in bag. Twist top of bag closed.
6. Fold several 15" lengths of raffia in half. Place fold of raffia at top of bag; wrap wire around folded raffia and top of bag to secure.
7. For hat, place funnel over top of bag.

*G*ifts from the garden are natural winners! For a fresh gift-giving alternative, share jars of flavor-packed Pickled Vegetables. The vine-ripened choices include mixed veggies seasoned with dill, and zucchini with oregano. Each jar is topped with a simple fabric square and nestled in a fabric-trimmed bag. Charming little garden stakes announce your offerings.

PICKLED VEGETABLES

14 pearl onions, peeled
14 cloves garlic
14 small chile peppers
5 medium zucchini
4 carrots
1 sweet red pepper
1 green pepper
   Fresh dill weed
   Fresh oregano
5 cups water
1½ cups white vinegar
6 tablespoons canning and pickling salt

Place 1 each of onions, garlic cloves, and chile peppers in 14 heat-resistant jars. Cut zucchini, carrots, and red and green peppers into 3½-inch strips. Pack a mixture of carrots, red and green peppers, sprigs of dill weed, and half of zucchini strips in 7 jars. Pack sprigs of oregano and remaining zucchini in remaining 7 jars. In a non-aluminum saucepan, combine water, vinegar, and canning salt over medium-high heat. Bring mixture to a boil. Carefully pour hot liquid over vegetables. Cover and cool to room temperature. Store in refrigerator.

Yield: about 14 half-pints (7 large or 14 small gifts)

GARDEN-FRESH BAGS AND JARS

For each bag, you will need a brown paper bag (we used small and lunch-size bags); garden-motif fabric to cover bag; paper-backed fusible web; natural excelsior; and the following items for sign: cream-colored paper, corrugated cardboard, small resin vegetable(s), desired length twig, black felt-tip pen with fine point, and a hot glue gun and glue sticks.

For each jar lid cover, you will need fabric and natural raffia.

1. For bag, follow manufacturer's instructions to fuse web to wrong side of fabric.
2. Cut a piece of fabric slightly smaller than front of bag; remove paper backing. Fuse fabric to bag.
3. For cuff on small bag, fold top of bag down about 1"; repeat. For cuff on lunch bag, fold top of bag down about 1½"; repeat twice.
4. Line bag with excelsior.
5. For sign, use black pen to write recipe name on a small piece of cream-colored paper. Cut a piece of cardboard slightly larger than paper piece. Glue paper piece to cardboard piece. Glue vegetable(s) to sign. Glue 1 end of twig to back of sign. Place sign in bag.
6. For jar lid cover, tear a square of fabric to fit over top of jar; fringe edges. Center fabric over jar and tie several lengths of raffia into a bow around jar and fabric; trim ends.

Lend a helping hand to new parents with a thoughtful gift of Beef and Barley Soup. Packed with meat, potatoes, carrots, and corn, this hearty dinner and a loaf of bread will be another welcome delivery! Our new baby bag, lined with a cozy receiving blanket, features fused-on motifs and a humorous blessing.

BEEF AND BARLEY SOUP

2 teaspoons salt
1 teaspoon ground black pepper
2 to 2 1/2 pound boneless beef chuck roast, fat trimmed
6 cups water
5 ribs celery, cut into 2-inch pieces
1 large onion, sliced
2 cloves garlic, chopped
2 cans (14 1/2 ounces each) vegetable broth
2 cups cubed potatoes
1 can (14.5 ounces) stewed tomatoes
1 3/4 cups sliced zucchini
1 1/2 cups sliced carrots
1 can (8 ounces) whole kernel yellow corn
1 jar (6 ounces) sliced mushrooms
1/2 cup uncooked pearl barley

Rub salt and pepper over roast. Place seasoned roast in a stockpot. Add 6 cups water, celery, onion, and garlic. Place over medium-high heat; bring to a boil. Cover and reduce heat to medium low; simmer about 2 hours or until meat is tender. When meat is cool enough to handle, remove from broth and cut into small pieces. Strain broth and discard vegetables. Return meat and broth to stockpot over medium-high heat. Add vegetable broth, potatoes, undrained tomatoes, zucchini, carrots, undrained corn, undrained mushrooms, and barley. When soup begins to boil, cover and reduce heat to low. Simmer 45 minutes to 1 hour or until vegetables and barley are tender. Serve hot. Store in an airtight container in refrigerator.

Yield: about 16 cups soup

NEW BABY GIFT BAG

You will need a large gift bag with handles; baby blanket to line bag; fabrics to cover bag and tag and for baby blanket appliqué; paper-backed fusible web; white and desired colors of paper for baby, banner, and tag (we used peach for baby and green for banner and tag); tracing paper; graphite transfer paper; colored pencils; black felt-tip pen with fine point; 1/4" hole punch; and a hot glue gun and glue sticks.

1. Remove handle from front of bag; set aside.
2. Follow manufacturer's instructions to fuse web to wrong sides of fabrics.
3. Measure height of bag; add 1". Measure width of bag. Cut a piece of fabric the determined measurements. Remove paper backing. Fuse fabric to front of bag, fusing excess fabric to inside top of bag.
4. Punch 2 holes through fabric over existing handle holes; replace handle.
5. Trace blanket, banner, baby, and desired tag pattern, page 118, onto tracing paper; cut out blanket and banner patterns.
6. Use patterns to cut blanket from fabric and banner from desired color of paper. Use black pen to write "Wishing you joy, happiness, and some sleep!" on banner.
7. Use transfer paper to transfer baby pattern onto desired color of paper. Use colored pencils to color cheeks, hair, and diaper and to add shading around edges of baby's body, face, arms, and legs. Use black pen to draw over all transferred lines. Cut out baby.
8. Remove paper backing from blanket. Fuse blanket to front of bag. Glue baby to bag over blanket. Glue banner to bag above baby.
9. For tag, use transfer paper to transfer tag pattern to center of a 2 1/8" x 3 1/8" piece of colored paper. Use a colored pencil to color transferred words. Use black pen to draw over transferred lines and to write message on tag. Fuse fabric to white paper. Glue tag to fabric-covered paper. Cutting about 1/4" from edges of tag, cut tag from fabric-covered paper. Glue tag to bag.
10. Line bag with blanket.

A FRUITFUL HOLIDAY SURPRISE

*Deliver elegant —
yet inexpensive — holiday
greetings to your favorite
families with these lavish
fruit-print bags packed
with Easy Cobbler Mix
and purchased pie filling.
The opulent totes can be
completed in an evening,
and the recipe yields four
fabulous gifts!*

EASY COBBLER MIX

   4   cups all-purpose flour
   4   cups sugar
   3/4 cup dry buttermilk powder
   3   tablespoons baking powder
   2   teaspoons salt
   4   cans (21 ounces each) fruit pie
         filling to give with mixes

In a large bowl, combine flour, sugar,
buttermilk powder, baking powder, and
salt. Place 2 cups plus 3 tablespoons
cobbler mix in each of 4 resealable
plastic bags. Store in refrigerator. Give
each bag of cobbler mix with 1 can of pie
filling and serving instructions.

Yield: about 8³/₄ cups mix (4 gifts)

To serve: Preheat oven to 350 degrees.
Melt ¹/₂ cup butter in a 7 x 11-inch
baking dish. Spoon pie filling over melted
butter. In a medium bowl, combine mix
and ³/₄ cup water. Pour over pie filling
(do not stir). Bake 38 to 43 minutes or
until crust is golden brown and a
toothpick inserted in center of crust
comes out clean. Serve warm.

Yield: 6 to 8 servings

FRUIT-PRINT BAG

For each bag, you will need a
medium-size brown gift bag with handles
removed, fruit-print wrapping paper,
¹/₂ yd of 3"w and 1 yd of ¹/₂"w wired gold
mesh ribbon, ¹/₄" hole punch, spray
adhesive, and a hot glue gun and glue
sticks.

1. To cover bag, cut a piece of wrapping
paper slightly smaller than front of bag.
Use spray adhesive to glue wrapping
paper to front of bag.

2. Punch holes for bag handle through
paper.
3. For handle, hot glue 3¹/₂" at each end
of 3"w ribbon to front and back of bag
between holes.
4. Cut a 10" length of ¹/₂"w ribbon.
Thread ribbon through holes in back of
bag and knot ends inside bag; trim ends.
5. Thread remaining ¹/₂"w ribbon through
holes in front of bag and tie into a bow at
front of bag; trim ends.

TEA LOVER'S LEMON SUGAR

*T*ea for two will be even
sweeter when you share a gift
of Lemon-Flavored Sugar. The
simple two-ingredient mix
is equally delicious stirred
into hot or cold beverages.
To make your offering one
that's sure to please, present
it in a fabric-covered lunch
sack that's decorated with
wrapping-paper cutouts, a
doily, and pretty ribbons.

LEMON-FLAVORED SUGAR

1 cup sugar
1 package (0.23 ounces)
     unsweetened lemonade-flavored
     soft drink mix

In a medium bowl, combine sugar and
soft drink mix. Give with serving
instructions.

Yield: about 1 cup flavored sugar (1 gift)

To serve: Stir 2 teaspoons flavored sugar
into 6 ounces hot or cold tea.

DAINTY TEACUP BAG

You will need a white lunch bag, fabric,
paper-backed fusible web, wrapping
paper with teacup motifs, 6" dia. paper
doily, 14" lengths of desired ribbons, and
a ¼" hole punch.

1. Follow manufacturer's instructions to
fuse web to wrong sides of fabric and
wrapping paper.

2. Cut a piece of fabric same size as front
of bag; remove paper backing. Fuse fabric
to bag.
3. Cut teacup motifs from wrapping
paper; remove paper backing. Arrange
teacups on bag and fuse in place.
4. Place gift in bag.

5. Fold top of bag about 2" to back.
6. Fold doily in half and place over top of
bag. Punching through all layers, punch 2
holes close together about 1" from center
top of bag. Thread ribbon lengths through
holes and tie into a bow at front of bag;
trim ends.

BANANA SPLIT KIT

*S*urprise new homeowners who've been moving and unpacking boxes all day with a refreshingly frivolous housewarming gift — cool banana splits! Decorated with banana-print fabric, rickrack, and a fruity "corsage," the gift bag is chock-full of our very best Banana Split Toppings, bananas, and whipped cream. You'll want to carry along a carton of ice cream so your friends can enjoy this treat right away!

BANANA SPLIT TOPPINGS

VERY STRAWBERRY SAUCE
  2 tablespoons cornstarch
  1/4 cup water
  1 jar (12 ounces) strawberry preserves
  1 package (10 ounces) frozen sweetened sliced strawberries, thawed
  1/2 cup sugar

Dissolve cornstarch in water in a small bowl. Combine preserves, strawberries, and sugar in a medium saucepan over medium-high heat; stir until well blended. Stir cornstarch mixture into fruit mixture. Stirring constantly, boil about 5 minutes or until mixture thickens. Store in an airtight container in refrigerator. Serve warm or cold.

Yield: about 2 1/2 cups sauce

CRUNCHY WALNUT SAUCE
  1/2 cup firmly packed brown sugar
  1 tablespoon cornstarch
  1 cup boiling water
  1 cup finely chopped walnuts, toasted
  1 tablespoon butter
    Dash of salt
  1 teaspoon butter flavoring

Combine brown sugar and cornstarch in a heavy medium saucepan. Stirring constantly over medium heat, gradually add boiling water. Add walnuts, butter, and salt; cook about 6 minutes or until mixture thickens. Remove from heat. Stir in butter flavoring. Store in an airtight container in refrigerator. Serve warm.

Yield: about 1 1/3 cups walnut sauce

CHOCOLATE SATIN SYRUP
  1 cup sugar
  1/2 cup cocoa
  1/4 teaspoon salt
  1 cup light corn syrup
  1/2 cup half and half
  3 tablespoons butter or margarine
  1 teaspoon vanilla extract

In a heavy medium saucepan, combine sugar, cocoa, and salt. Add corn syrup, half and half, and butter. Stirring constantly, cook over medium heat 5 to 7 minutes or until sugar dissolves. Remove from heat; stir in vanilla. Store in an airtight container in refrigerator. Serve warm or cold.

Yield: about 2 2/3 cups chocolate sauce

BANANA SPLIT BAG

You will need a large white gift bag; banana-motif fabric; paper-backed fusible web; 1 1/4 yds of 1 3/8"w wired ribbon; 1 1/2 yds of 7/8"w satin ribbon; jumbo rickrack; ice cream scoop; artificial cherry, strawberry, banana, peanut, and pecan floral picks; floral wire; wire cutters; a 5 1/4" x 8" piece of white paper for card; and a hot glue gun and glue sticks.

1. Follow manufacturer's instructions to fuse web to wrong side of fabric. Cut a piece of fabric about 1 1/2" smaller on all sides than front of bag. Remove paper backing. Center and fuse fabric to front of bag.
2. Glue lengths of rickrack along edges of fabric.
3. Cut one 3" and one 6" length of satin ribbon; set aside.
4. Holding wired ribbon and remaining satin ribbon together, follow *Making a Multi-Loop Bow*, page 123, to form a bow without bow center. For bow center, fold 3" satin ribbon length in half lengthwise and wrap around center of bow; glue ends at back to secure. Glue a 3" length of rickrack around bow center.
5. Glue stems of fruit and nut picks to back of bow. Glue bow to bag. Glue handle of ice cream scoop to bag near bow.
6. For card, match short edges and fold white paper piece in half. Use small dots of glue to glue 6" satin ribbon length to front of card about 1" from fold; trim ends even with edges of card. Cut a banana motif from fused fabric; remove paper backing and fuse to front of card over ribbon. Glue a length of rickrack to front of card; trim ends even with edges of card.

PRETTY PICNIC-IN-A-BAG

*T*he next time you invite the girls "out" for lunch, impress them with a fabulous picnic-in-a-bag! Packed with single servings of Curried Chicken Salad, crackers, and fresh fruit, each bag is beautifully decorated with a matching paper napkin and plate and plastic utensils.

CURRIED CHICKEN SALAD

  4 cups chopped cooked chicken
  1 can (15$1/4$ ounces) pineapple tidbits, drained
$1/2$ cup finely chopped green onions
$1/2$ cup finely chopped dry-roasted peanuts
$1/4$ cup finely chopped sweet red pepper
$1/4$ cup finely chopped golden raisins
$3/4$ cup mayonnaise
  2 teaspoons curry powder
$1/2$ teaspoon ground ginger
$1/2$ teaspoon salt
$1/2$ teaspoon ground white pepper

In a large bowl, combine chicken, pineapple, onions, peanuts, red pepper, and raisins. In a small bowl, combine mayonnaise, curry powder, ginger, salt, and white pepper. Fold mayonnaise mixture into chicken mixture. Store in an airtight container in refrigerator.

Yield: about 6 cups chicken salad (6 gifts)

PICNIC BAG

For each bag, you will need a white gift bag, matching paper plate and napkin, plastic utensils, $1/2$ yd of $7/8$"w wired ribbon, 8" of $1/8$"w satin ribbon, $1/8$" hole punch, white and colored paper for tag, black felt-tip pen with fine point, and a craft glue stick.

1. For cuff, fold top of bag down about $1^{1}/2$"; repeat. Fold napkin diagonally over top front of bag.
2. Punching through all layers, punch 2 holes about $1/2$" and 1" from center top of front of bag. Thread wired ribbon through holes and tie into a bow around utensils at front of bag; trim ends. Arrange utensils as desired.
3. Place plate and lunch in bag.
4. For tag, cut a $1^{1}/2$" x $3^{1}/4$" piece of white paper. Use black pen to write "Lunch!" on tag. Use glue stick to glue tag to colored paper. Cutting close to tag, cut tag from colored paper. Punch a hole in tag. Thread tag onto satin ribbon; knot ribbon ends. Hang tag on 1 utensil.

94

SWIRLS OF FUN

Perfect party favors for your child's birthday guests, Fun Cookie Suckers are swirls of fun! Sunday-morning funny papers and colorful shoelaces transform purchased polka-dot gift bags into lighthearted carriers. Every child will go home feeling like a special birthday honoree!

FUN COOKIE SUCKERS

- 3/4 cup butter or margarine, softened
- 1 package (3 ounces) cream cheese, softened
- 1 cup sugar
- 1 egg
- 1 teaspoon vanilla extract
- 2 3/4 cups all-purpose flour
- 1 teaspoon baking powder
- 1/4 teaspoon salt
  Pink, blue, green, and orange paste food coloring
  Lollipop sticks

In a large bowl, cream butter, cream cheese, and sugar until fluffy. Add egg and vanilla; beat until smooth. In a medium bowl, combine flour, baking powder, and salt. Add dry ingredients to creamed mixture; stir until a soft dough forms. Divide dough into fourths; tint pink, blue, green, and orange. Divide each color in half; wrap in plastic wrap and chill 2 hours.

Preheat oven to 350 degrees. Working with half of each color dough at a time, shape dough into 3/4-inch balls. For each cookie, place 1 pink, blue, green, and

orange ball together to make 1 large ball. Shape into a 12-inch-long roll. Starting at one end, coil roll to make about a 2 3/4-inch-diameter cookie. Place cookies 3 inches apart on a lightly greased baking sheet. Carefully insert lollipop sticks into bottoms of cookies. Bake 8 to 10 minutes or until bottoms are lightly browned. Transfer cookies to a wire rack to cool. Store in an airtight container.

Yield: about 2 1/2 dozen cookies (15 gifts)

COMIC BAG

For each bag, you will need a small flat polka-dot gift bag, color newspaper comics, multicolor shoelace, colored paper for tag, black felt-tip pen with medium point, tracing paper, 1/4" hole punch, and craft glue.

1. Cut desired panel(s) from comics. Glue panel(s) to front of bag.
2. Place gift in bag. Fold top of bag about 1 1/2" to front. Punch 2 holes close together at center of folded part of bag.
3. Thread shoelace through holes and tie into a bow at front of bag.
4. For tag, trace pattern, page 119, onto tracing paper; cut out. Use pattern to cut tag from colored paper. Use black pen to write name on tag. Glue tag to 1 end of shoelace.

F or all the times she's been there, show a dear friend how special she is to you with this sweet surprise! Our simply decorated Hand-in-Hand Cookies are even more engaging when presented in a sack that's embellished with fused-on fabric cutouts.

HAND-IN-HAND COOKIES

COOKIES

- 1/2 cup butter or margarine, softened
- 3/4 cup granulated sugar
- 1/4 cup firmly packed brown sugar
- 1 egg
- 1 teaspoon vanilla extract
- 1/4 teaspoon orange extract
- 2 cups all-purpose flour
- 2 teaspoons baking powder
- 1/2 teaspoon salt

ICING

- 3/4 cup plus 2 tablespoons sifted confectioners sugar
- 1 tablespoon cocoa
- 1 1/2 to 2 tablespoons milk
- 1/4 teaspoon vanilla extract

For cookies, cream butter and sugars in a medium bowl until fluffy. Add egg and extracts; beat until smooth. In a small bowl, combine flour, baking powder, and salt. Add dry ingredients to creamed mixture; stir until well blended. Divide dough into fourths. Wrap in plastic wrap and chill 1 hour.

Preheat oven to 400 degrees. On a lightly floured surface, use a floured rolling pin to roll out one fourth of dough to about 1/8-inch thickness and about a 6 1/2-inch square. For neat edges, trim dough into a 6-inch square; reserve dough scraps. Cut 2 x 3-inch cookies. Place 1 inch apart on a lightly greased baking sheet. Bake 4 to 6 minutes or until edges are lightly browned. Transfer cookies to a wire rack to cool. Repeat with remaining dough.

For icing, combine confectioners sugar, cocoa, milk, and vanilla in a small bowl; stir until smooth. Spoon icing into a pastry bag fitted with a small round tip. Pipe stick-figure girls onto cookies with hands meeting at sides. Allow icing to harden. Store in an airtight container.

Yield: about 2 dozen cookies (2 gifts)

"FRIENDS FOREVER" BAG

For each bag, you will need a medium-size gift bag with handles removed; fabrics for appliqué background, appliqués, bow, and card; paper-backed fusible web; 3 small black beads for buttons on dress; 1/4 yd of 1/8"w satin ribbon; 3/4" dia. button; embroidery floss to coordinate with fabrics; a 3 1/4" x 5 1/2" piece of brown paper; brown felt-tip pen with fine point; pink colored pencil; a 1/4" hole punch (if necessary); and a hot glue gun and glue sticks.

1. For appliqué background, tear a piece of fabric about 1" narrower and 2" shorter than bag front; fringe edges. Follow manufacturer's instructions to fuse web to wrong side of fabric. Remove paper backing. Center and fuse fabric about 1/2" from bottom on front of bag.
2. Use patterns, this page and page 119, and follow *Making Appliqués,* page 122, to make 2 heads, 2 dresses, and letters to spell "FRIENDS FOREVER" from fabrics. Remove paper backing. Arrange appliqués on background; fuse in place.
3. Use pink pencil to color cheeks. Use brown pen to draw eyes, hair, arms, legs, and dashed lines about 1/8" inside edges of faces and dresses and just outside edges of background fabric to resemble stitching.
4. Tie ribbon into a bow; trim ends. Glue bow and beads to dresses.
5. Place gift in bag.
6. For bow at top of bag, punch 2 holes about 3" apart close to center top of bag if necessary (bag may already have holes where handles were removed). Tear a 1" x 10" strip of fabric; thread strip through holes in top of bag and knot at back. Tear two 1" x 20" strips of fabric. Tie strips together into a bow. Glue bow to top of bag. Trim ends of fabric strips.
7. For card, tear a 2 3/4" x 5" piece of fabric. Fuse web to wrong side of fabric. Remove paper backing. Center and fuse fabric to brown paper. With paper side up and short edges at top and bottom, fold bottom edge of paper up 2 1/4"; fold top edge down 1" to form a flap. Thread a length of embroidery floss through button and tie into a bow at front; trim ends. Glue button to flap of card. Punch a hole in top left corner of card. Loop a length of floss through hole and tie card to bow on bag.

HEAD

DRESS

97

Give your hostess a soothing way to pause and unwind after the party with our Spiced Cranberry Tea Mix. All she has to do is add hot water and stir! For a fun presentation, pack this tea-time gift in a giant "tea bag." Made with interfacing and fusible web tape, the bag won't even require a trip to the sewing machine!

SPICED CRANBERRY TEA MIX

- 1 cup unsweetened powdered instant tea
- 1 cup sugar
- 1/2 cup orange-flavored powdered instant breakfast drink
- 2 packages (3 ounces each) cranberry gelatin
- 1 teaspoon ground cinnamon
- 1 teaspoon ground allspice

Process all ingredients in a food processor until well blended. Store in a resealable plastic bag. Give with serving instructions.

Yield: about 2 1/2 cups mix (1 gift)

To serve: Pour 6 ounces hot water over 2 tablespoons tea mix; stir until well blended.

"TEA-RRIFIC" TEA BAG

You will need a 12" x 15 1/2" piece of medium-weight non-woven interfacing for bag, 1/2"w paper-backed fusible web tape, white and red paper, a 2" x 5 1/2" piece of cardboard, 9" of cotton twine, 2 paper clips for "staples," wire cutters, red and black felt-tip pens with fine points, tracing paper, serrated-cut craft scissors, 1/8" hole punch, pressing cloth, and a hot glue gun and glue sticks.

1. (*Note:* Use pressing cloth for Steps 1 - 4.) Referring to Fig. 1, press 1" pleats about 3" from each short edge of interfacing (inside is wrong side of interfacing; creases will be used later to form sides of bag); unfold interfacing.

Fig. 1

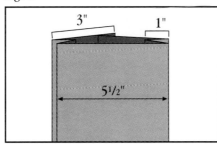

2. Follow manufacturer's instructions to fuse web tape along 1 short edge and 1 long edge (bottom) on wrong side of interfacing; remove paper backing.
3. Place interfacing wrong side up. Fold short edges 4" to center, overlapping fused short edge over unfused short edge. Fuse overlapped edges and bottom edges of bag together (overlap is center back of bag).
4. Fuse web tape along bottom edge on back of bag. Press bottom edge 1" to back of bag. Unfold edge and remove paper backing. Refold edge and fuse in place. Repeat on front bottom edge of bag.
5. Open bag and flatten at bottom, using creases pressed in Step 1 to form sides of bag. Trimming to fit if necessary, place

cardboard piece in bottom of bag. Fold bottom corners of bag up and glue to sides of bag.
6. Place gift in bag.
7. For "staples" on tea bag and label, use wire cutters to remove small center "hook" from each paper clip (Fig. 2).

Fig. 2

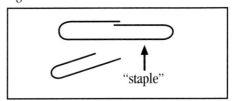
"staple"

8. With sides of bag creased and top front and back of bag together, fold top corners of bag about 1 1/2" to back. Fold top edge of bag about 1 1/4" to back. Punch 2 holes about 1" apart at center of bag about 1" from top fold. Insert ends of 1 "staple" through holes in bag.
9. For tea bag label, cut a 2 1/2" x 3" piece of red paper. Use craft scissors to cut a 2 1/4" x 2 5/8" piece of white paper. Use red pen to write "SPICED CRANBERRY TEA MIX" on white paper piece. Punch 2 holes about 1" apart near 1 short edge of red paper piece. Glue white paper piece to red paper piece below holes. Insert ends of remaining "staple" through holes. Glue 1 end of twine to front of tag under "staple." Pass remaining end of twine under "staple" on bag and glue end to back of bag.
10. For tag, trace spoon pattern onto tracing paper; cut out. Use pattern to cut spoon from red paper. Use black pen to draw along edges and to write "THANKS! YOU'RE A TEA-RRIFIC HOSTESS!" on spoon. Glue spoon to bag.

SASSY BARBECUE SAUCE

The next time you're invited to a cookout, surprise the host with a gift of sassy Bourbon Barbecue Sauce! The fiery blend combines onions, jalapeño peppers, and bourbon in a sweet tomato base. For a gift with sizzle, pack the sauce in a blue jean-inspired bag along with grilling utensils and a handy mitt.

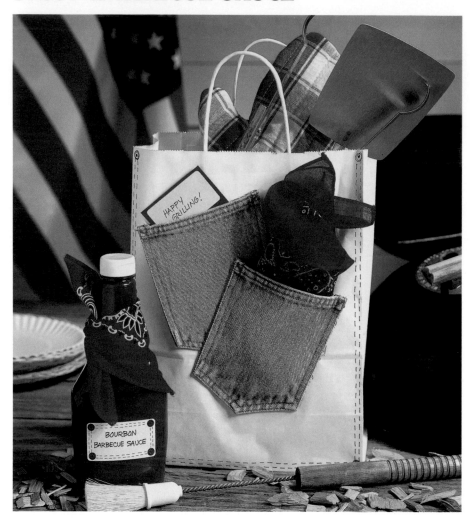

BOURBON BARBECUE SAUCE

$^1/_2$ cup butter or margarine
1$^1/_4$ cups finely chopped onions
  1 to 2 fresh jalapeño peppers, seeded and finely chopped
  2 cloves garlic, minced
  4 cups ketchup
  2 tablespoons apple cider vinegar
  2 tablespoons Worcestershire sauce
  1 cup firmly packed brown sugar
  1 teaspoon dry mustard
$^1/_2$ cup bourbon

In a small Dutch oven, melt butter over medium-high heat. Sauté onions, jalapeño peppers, and garlic in butter about 5 minutes or until tender. Reduce heat to medium-low. Stir in ketchup, vinegar, and Worcestershire sauce. Add brown sugar and dry mustard; stir until well blended. Stirring frequently, cook 10 minutes. Stir in bourbon; cook about 3 minutes or until mixture is heated through. Store in an airtight container in refrigerator.

Yield: about 6 cups sauce (2 gifts)

BARBECUE GIFT BAG

For each gift, we filled an empty 24-ounce ketchup bottle with the sauce and decorated the bottle with a label and a corner cut from a bandanna.

For each bag, you will need a large white gift bag, 2 back pockets cut from old blue jeans, red bandanna, a 3" x 3$^1/_2$" red paper piece and a 1$^1/_2$" x 2$^3/_4$" self-adhesive label for tag, black felt-tip pen with fine point, and a hot glue gun and glue sticks.

1. With bag flattened, use black pen to draw small circles in each corner on front of bag to resemble rivets on jeans. Draw 2 dashed lines about $^1/_4$" apart between circles along side and bottom edges of bag to resemble stitching.
2. Arrange pockets on bag and glue in place.
3. Tuck bandanna into 1 pocket.
4. For tag, use black pen to write message on label. Adhere label close to 1 long edge of red paper piece. Tuck tag in remaining pocket.

FETCHING DOGGIE BAG

*E*ven the pickiest pooch will love home-baked treats made with our special mix! To create a fetching gift for a new pet owner, dress up a brown bag with raffia, a bone-shaped cookie cutter, and puppy cutouts. This package is so "doggone" cute that both owner and canine will howl with delight!

SPECIAL DOG TREAT MIX

- 2 cups whole-wheat flour
- 1 cup all-purpose flour
- 1 cup yellow cornmeal
- 1/2 cup nonfat dry milk powder
- 1/2 teaspoon garlic powder
- 1 package (3 ounces) beef jerky dog treats, finely chopped
- 1/2 cup shredded Cheddar cheese

In a large bowl, combine flours, cornmeal, dry milk, and garlic powder. Stir in beef pieces and cheese. Store in an airtight container in refrigerator. Give with recipe for Special Dog Treats.

Yield: about 5 cups mix (2 gifts)

SPECIAL DOG TREATS

- 2 1/2 cups Special Dog Treat Mix
- 1/3 cup vegetable oil
- 1/4 cup plus 2 tablespoons beef or chicken broth
- 1 egg

Preheat oven to 300 degrees. In a large bowl, combine mix, oil, broth, and egg; stir until well blended. On a lightly floured surface, pat dough to 3/8-inch thickness. Use a 1 7/8 x 3 5/8-inch bone-shaped cookie cutter to cut out treats. Transfer to an ungreased baking sheet. Bake 20 to 22 minutes or until firm and bottoms are lightly browned. Transfer treats to a wire rack to cool. Store in an airtight container in refrigerator.

Yield: about 1 dozen dog treats

DOGGIE TREAT BAG

For each bag, you will need a medium-size brown gift bag, a 1 7/8" x 3 5/8" bone-shaped cookie cutter, black paper, kraft paper, natural raffia, 16" of jute twine, tracing paper, black felt-tip pen with fine point, 1/4" hole punch, craft glue stick, and a hot glue gun and glue sticks.

1. Trace patterns, page 120, onto tracing paper; cut out. Use patterns to cut dogs and small bones from black paper and large bone from kraft paper.

2. Use glue stick to glue begging dog to left side of front of bag; glue square end of remaining dog to inside of bag front at top of bag.

3. Tie several lengths of raffia into a bow; trim ends. Hot glue bow to bag; glue small bones to bow.

4. Place gift in bag. Hot glue top of bag closed.

5. Punch a hole at center top of bag. Tie jute around cookie cutter. Thread 1 end of jute through hole in bag. Knot ends of jute at back of bag.

6. For tag, use black pen to write "Doggie Treats" on large bone. Use glue stick to glue large bone to black paper. Cutting close to bone, cut bone from black paper. Hot glue tag to bag.

FOR THE BIRDS

A simple combination of kitchen staples and bird seed, this mix is sure to attract a flock of feathered friends! It's a natural gift choice for friends who are cuckoo about bird-watching. For fun, present the "tweet" treat in terra-cotta saucers so it can be set out immediately!

BIRD-WATCHING MIX

  1   cup bacon drippings
  1   cup cornmeal
  ¼   cup molasses or corn syrup
  ¼   cup fruit preserves
  1   cup peanut butter
  1   cup mixed wild bird seed

In a heavy medium saucepan, melt bacon drippings over medium heat. Remove from heat. Stir in cornmeal, molasses, and preserves. Add peanut butter and bird seed; stir until well blended. Spread a heaping cup of mixture into each of three 4½-inch-diameter plant saucers. Cover and store in a cool place.

Yield: about 3½ cups bird mix (3 gifts)

BIRD-WATCHING GIFT BAG

For each bag, you will need a medium-size gift bag with bird-motifs, a 1³⁄₈" x 3½" paper piece for tag, 20" of ⁷⁄₈"w ribbon, a bird feather (available at craft stores), brown felt-tip calligraphy pen with medium point, and a ¼" hole punch.

1. If bag has handles, trim top edge of bag away just below handles.
2. Lay bag on its back and place gift in bag.
3. For flap, fold top of bag about 1¼" to front.
4. Punch 2 holes about 1" apart at center of folded part of bag.

5. Thread ribbon through holes and tie into a bow at front of bag; trim ends. Tuck feather behind knot of bow.
6. For tag, use brown pen to write "Happy Bird-Watching!" on paper piece. Tuck tag under bag flap.

SUNFLOWER BATH BASKET

*S*unflowers are all the rage in home decorating, so we teamed the saffron blossoms with easy-to-make scented oil for a fashionable bath basket. You can present the bath oil along with a decorated bag filled with scented soaps. Add a bath sponge and some nice new towels, and you'll have a "blooming" gift that a friend will love!

BATH OIL

You will need a 12-ounce decorative bottle with cork, almond oil to fill bottle, lemon essential oil (available at health food stores), a 3¼" dia. silk sunflower, and 20" of ⅝"w wired white ribbon.

1. Fill bottle with almond oil. Add 24 drops of lemon essential oil to almond oil. Firmly insert cork into bottle.
2. Tie ribbon into a bow around neck of bottle; trim ends. Glue sunflower to ribbon.

SUNFLOWER BAG

You will need a white lunch bag, fabric, a 4" dia. silk sunflower, paper-backed fusible web, stapler, aluminum foil, and a hot glue gun and glue sticks.

1. Follow manufacturer's instructions to fuse web to wrong side of fabric. Cut a piece of fabric slightly smaller than front of bag; remove paper backing. Fuse fabric to front of bag.

2. Take flower apart, discarding any plastic or metal pieces; set aside flower center. Use a warm, dry iron to press bottom section of petals flat.
3. Place a piece of foil shiny side up on ironing board. Place petal section wrong side up on foil. Lay a piece of web paper side up over petal section. Follow manufacturer's instructions to fuse web to wrong side of petal section. Remove and save paper backing. Peel petal section

from foil. Trim excess web from petal section.
4. Center petal section on back of flattened bag about ½" from top. Fuse petal section in place, using saved paper backing as a pressing cloth. Trim top of bag close to petals.
5. Place gift in bag.
6. Fold top of bag about 3" to front and staple bag closed at center of petal section. Glue flower center over staple.

103

FUN WITH PLAY DOUGH

*F*eaterthe *featuring fruity scents, our homemade play dough makes a wonderful gift for an artistic preschooler. This gift is sure to inspire young imaginations when delivered with a mini rolling pin and fun-shaped cookie cutters. A vinyl place mat makes a handy carry-all that doubles as a portable play station!*

FRUITY PLAY DOUGH

For a variety of colors, make several recipes using different flavors of soft drink mixes.

- 1 cup all-purpose flour
- 1/2 cup salt
- 2 teaspoons cream of tartar
- 1 package (about 0.13 ounces) unsweetened soft drink mix (we used lemonade tinted with yellow food coloring, cherry, lemon-lime, orange, and grape)
- 1 cup boiling water
- 1 tablespoon vegetable oil

Combine flour, salt, cream of tartar, and soft drink mix in a medium bowl. Add boiling water and oil; stir until a soft dough forms. (If using lemonade soft drink mix, tint yellow.) Knead mixture until smooth. Store in an airtight container in refrigerator.

Yield: about 2 cups play dough (fills about 9 paint cups)

PLACE MAT PLAY BAG

For each bag, you will need a 12" x 18" vinyl place mat, two 13" lengths of wired vinyl ribbon, 1/2 yd of 1/8"w satin ribbon,

two 81/4" lengths of 3/4"w self-adhesive hook and loop fastener tape, colored paper for tag, assorted colors of felt-tip pens, hot glue gun and glue sticks, plastic cookie cutters, 11/2-ounce plastic paint cups with lids, and a miniature rolling pin.

1. Separate lengths of hook and loop fastener tape and adhere to wrong side of place mat (Fig. 1).

Fig. 1

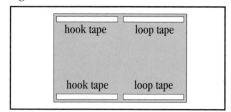

2. For handles, fold ends of each vinyl ribbon length 1/2" to 1 side (wrong side). Glue handles to wrong side of place mat (Fig. 2).

Fig. 2

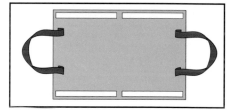

3. For tag, use a pencil to draw around a cookie cutter on paper; cut out shape. Use colored pens to write message and decorate shape. Glue shape to cookie cutter. Cut 1/8"w ribbon length in half. Tie 1 length of ribbon into a bow; trim ends. Glue bow to tag. Wrap remaining length of ribbon around 1 handle of bag; glue ribbon ends to back of tag to secure.
4. Fold bag in half and fasten hook and loop tape.
5. Fill paint cups with Fruity Play Dough. Place cups, rolling pin, and additional cookie cutters in bag.

CANDLELIGHT ROSES

*R*oses and candlelight always set a romantic mood, so we paired the two with this exquisite candle for a bride-to-be. The candle is adorned with dried rosebuds, and the rose-inspired bag is made from a strip of sheer fabric.

EMBELLISHED CANDLE

You will need a 2¹/₂" dia. x 6"h ivory pillar candle, Candle Magic® Wax Stick-ums, Ivory Lace Candle Magic® Wax Crystals (we used about three 12-ounce packages of crystals; melted crystals can be used to dip several candles), dried miniature rosebuds, small coffee can for melting wax, pan to hold can, newspapers, and waxed paper.

1. Use Wax Stick-ums to attach rosebuds to candle.
2. (*Caution:* Do not melt wax over an open flame or directly on burner.) Cover work area with newspaper. Place wax crystals in can. Place can in pan; fill pan half full with water. Heat water until wax crystals melt.
3. Dip candle in melted wax. Allowing wax to harden slightly between coats, continue dipping candle in wax until desired covering is achieved.
4. Place candle on waxed paper to cool.

ROSETTE BAG

You will need a 7" x 44" strip of sheer fabric, Kreinik® silver (001) fine (#8) braid, corsage pins, 2 silk leaves with wire stems, ivory paper, miniature dried rosebud, drawing compass, pink felt-tip

pen with fine point, ¹/₈" hole punch, and a hot glue gun and glue sticks.

1. Match wrong sides and short edges and fold fabric strip in half. Beginning at fold and using a ¹/₂" seam allowance, use a double strand of silver braid to work running stitch along each side of fabric strip (Fig. 1). Pull braid slightly to gather each side of bag; knot ends of braid. Fray edges of bag next to stitched lines.

Fig. 1

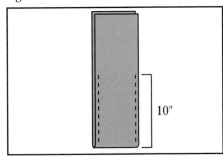

2. Place candle in bag.
3. Loosely twisting ends of fabric strip together above candle, wrap ends in a circle from center out to form a rosette; tuck raw edges of fabric under rosette. Secure rosette with corsage pins. Wrap stems of leaves around base of rosette to secure.
4. For tag, use compass to draw a 2" dia. circle on ivory paper; cut out. Punch a hole in tag. Glue rosebud to tag. Use pink pen to personalize tag. Cut two 10" lengths of braid. Thread braid through hole in tag and knot ends together about 2" from ends. Loop braid around base of rosette on bag.

FRESH SCENT SOAP

A bottle of aromatic soap makes a refreshing appreciation gift, especially when you add your own hand-colored label! The fresh-scented cleanser features a fragrant blend of three essential oils. For added elegance, present your surprise in a brown lunch sack trimmed with a matching tag and sparkling ribbons.

FRESH SCENT SOAP

You will need a 12-ounce bottle of clear liquid soap (we used Ivory-Free® liquid soap); lavender, lemon, and spearmint essential oils (available at health food stores); a photocopy of label design (page 115); green colored pencil; black felt-tip pen with fine point; clear self-adhesive plastic (we used Con-Tact® paper); and adhesive remover (if needed).

1. Remove existing label(s) from soap bottle; if necessary, use adhesive remover to remove any adhesive residue.
2. In a small bowl, mix 6 drops of each essential oil with liquid soap; stir well. Return scented soap to bottle.
3. For label, use green pencil to color leaves and shade border of photocopied label. Use black pen to personalize label. Cut out label.
4. Use a pencil to draw around label on paper side of self-adhesive plastic. Cutting about 1/4" outside drawn oval, cut out oval. Remove paper backing. Carefully center label right side down on adhesive side of plastic; center label on bottle and smooth in place.

IVY BAG

You will need a brown lunch bag, 3/4 yd of 3"w wired gold mesh ribbon, 20" of 1 1/2"w wired iridescent green ribbon, 3/4 yd of 1/4"w gold ribbon, a photocopy of label design (page 115), a 3 3/4" x 5 1/4" green paper piece for tag, green colored pencil, black felt-tip pen with fine point, craft glue stick, and a 1/4" hole punch.

1. Place bottle in bag.
2. With ends at top, wrap 3"w ribbon lengthwise around center of bag. Tie 1 1/2"w ribbon into a bow around top of bag and ends of wide ribbon; trim ends.
3. For card, follow Step 3 of Fresh Scent Soap instructions. Match short edges and fold green paper piece in half. Use glue stick to glue label to center front of card. Punch a hole in corner of card. Thread 1/4"w ribbon through hole and tie into a bow around bow on bag.

SCENTED FIRE STARTERS

*F*riends who love a glowing fire will appreciate your thoughtful holiday wishes — especially when delivered with a bag of scented fire starters made using tinted paraffin and pinecones. For a gift that will warm their hearts as well as their homes, pack the Christmasy cones in a rustic burlap bag that's finished with a jumbo jingle bell and a hand-colored tag.

SCENTED PINECONE FIRE STARTERS

You will need pinecones, paraffin, either red and green candle pieces or crayons, desired candle scent, coffee cans, cooking pan, newspaper, waxed paper, and tongs.

1. (*Caution:* Do not melt paraffin over an open flame or directly on burner.) Cover work area with newspaper. Place coffee can in pan filled with water. Heat paraffin in can until melted. Add pieces of red or green candles or crayons to melted paraffin until desired color is achieved. Add candle scent to melted paraffin.
2. Use tongs to dip pinecones in melted paraffin. Allowing paraffin to harden slightly between coats, continue dipping pinecones in paraffin until desired covering is achieved. Place pinecones on waxed paper to cool.

BURLAP BAG

You will need a 10" x 26" piece of burlap, thread to match burlap, red and green yarn, large needle, silk holly sprig, large jingle bell, photocopy of tag design (page 123), red paper, colored pencils, a ⅛" hole punch, and a craft glue stick.

1. Follow Steps 2, 3, and 5 of *Making a Sewn Fabric Bag*, page 122, to make bag from burlap. Fringe top edge of bag about ¼".
2. For tag, use colored pencils to color photocopy. Cut out tag. Glue tag to red paper. Cutting close to tag, cut tag from red paper. Punch a hole in 1 corner of tag.
3. Cut a 26" length of each yarn color. Thread both lengths onto needle. Beginning and ending at front of bag and threading jingle bell onto yarn at 1 side of bag, work a running stitch around top of bag about 1½" from fringed edges. Thread tag onto yarn. Tie yarn lengths into a bow to close bag. Tuck holly sprig under bow.

PATTERNS

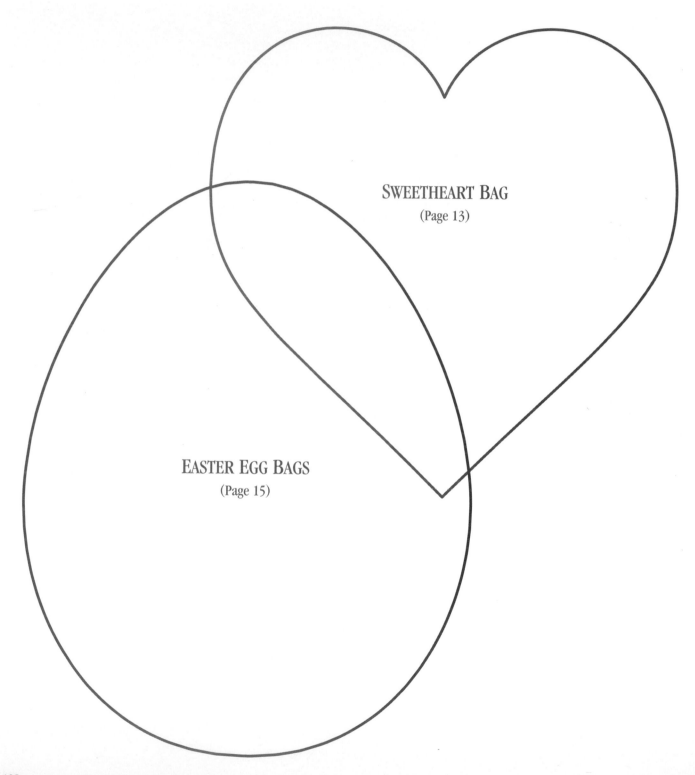

SWEETHEART BAG

(Page 13)

EASTER EGG BAGS

(Page 15)

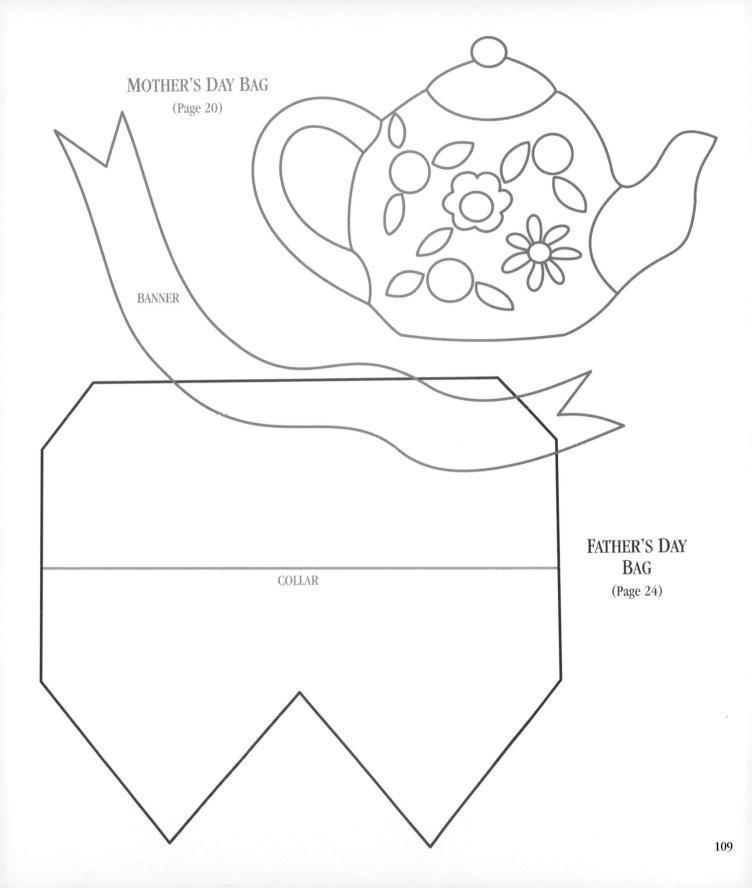

MOTHER'S DAY BAG
(Page 20)

BANNER

COLLAR

FATHER'S DAY
BAG
(Page 24)

PATTERNS (continued)

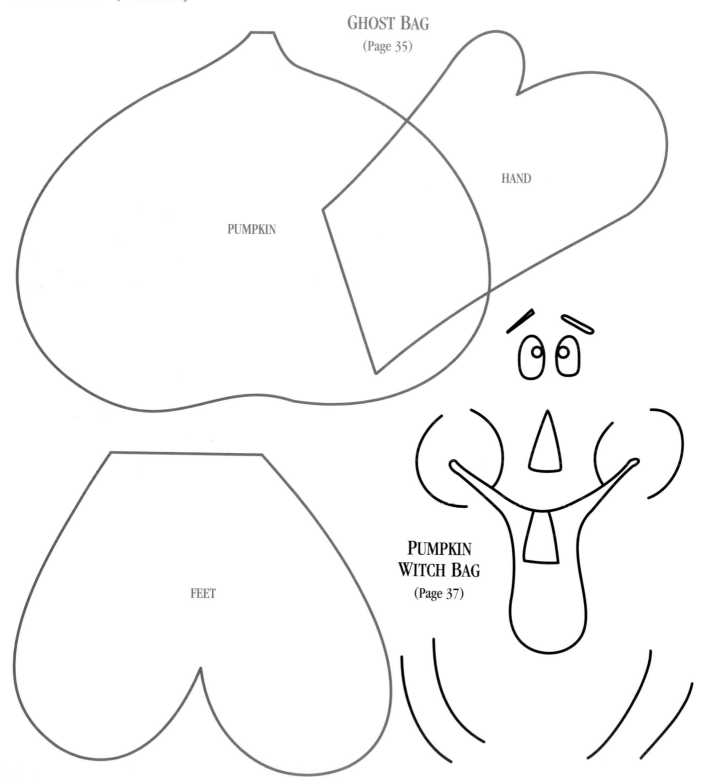

GHOST BAG
(Page 35)

HAND

PUMPKIN

FEET

PUMPKIN
WITCH BAG
(Page 37)

OVALS

SANTA'S SACKS
(Page 43)

"HO-HO-HO" BAG
(Page 48)

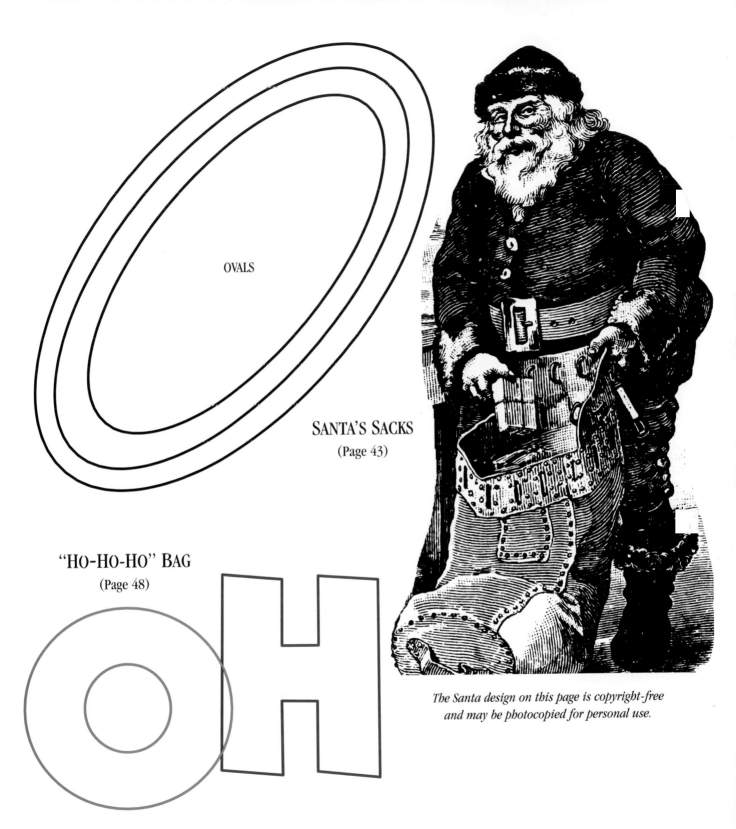

*The Santa design on this page is copyright-free
and may be photocopied for personal use.*

PATTERNS (continued)

NOSE

SNOWMAN BAG
(Page 49)

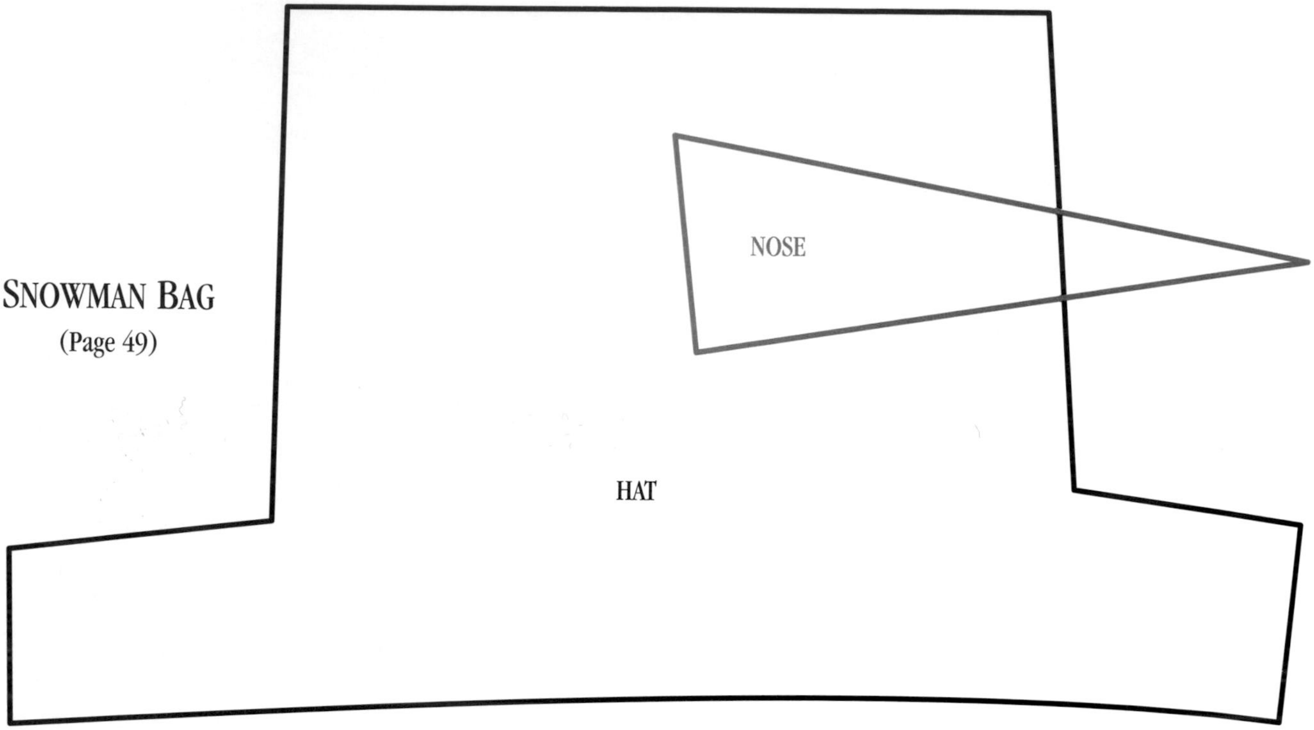

HAT

GINGERBREAD BOYS

FLOWER CENTER

FLOWER

GINGERBREAD BOY BAG
(Page 57)

HEART

SPRINGTIME FLOWERS BAG
(Page 59)

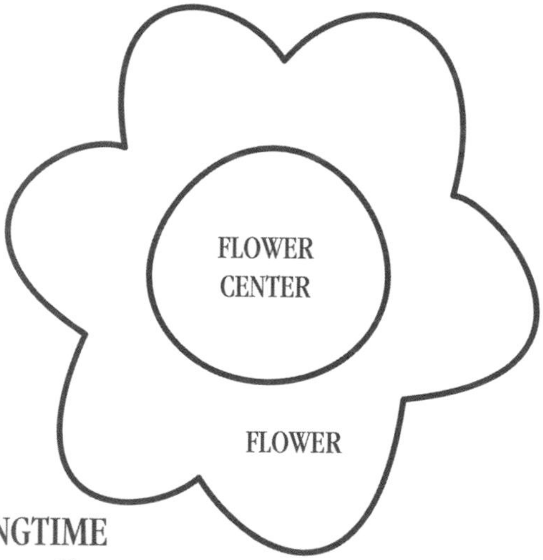

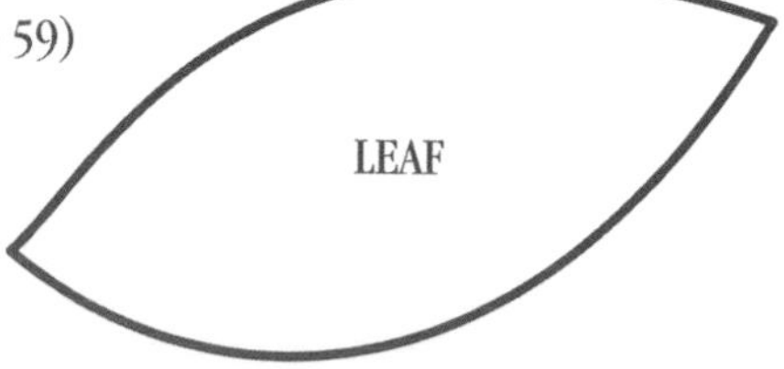

LEAF

CHEESE MIX GIFT CARD

(Page 55)

The Santa and label designs on this page are copyright-free and may be photocopied for personal use.

A MERRY CHRISTMAS

Boursin Cheese Spread
Combine 2 Tbsp. mix with
16 oz. softened cream
cheese; beat until well
blended.
Serve with crackers.

LEAVES

FLOWER CENTER

FLOWER

FELT FLOWER MAGNET BAG

(Page 60)

PATTERNS (continued)

"THANK YOU" BAG
(Page 63)

LEAF

FLOWER
CENTER

FLOWER

ANGEL BAG
(Page 65)

thanks you're an Angel

Leisure Arts, Inc., grants permission to the owner of this book to photocopy the label design on this page for personal use only.

FRESH SCENT SOAP AND IVY BAG
(Page 106)

Fresh Scent Liquid Soap

PATTERNS (continued)

STENCILED MUSLIN BAG
(Page 70)

STENCIL CUTTING KEY
- ☑ Stencil #1
- ☑ Stencil #2

COLOR KEY
Stencil #1 — yellow shaded with red
Stencil #2 — green

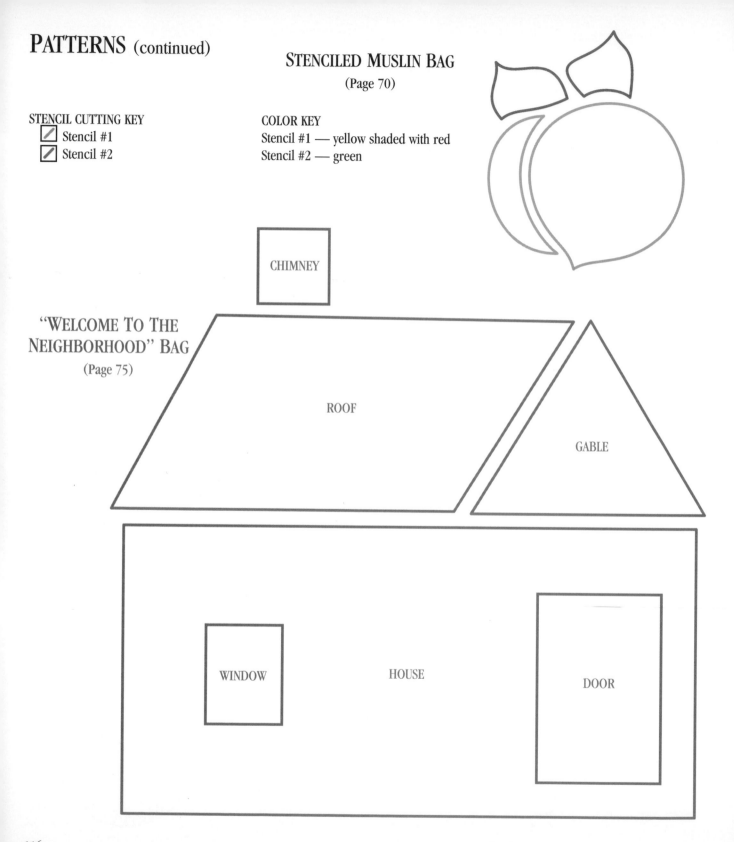

"WELCOME TO THE NEIGHBORHOOD" BAG
(Page 75)

CHIMNEY

ROOF

GABLE

WINDOW

HOUSE

DOOR

"HOMEMADE"
BOTTLE BAG
(Page 83)

PIZZA KIT BASKET

(Page 77)

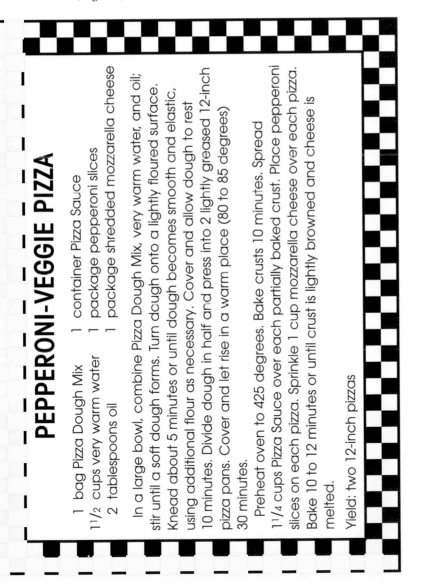

PEPPERONI-VEGGIE PIZZA

1 bag Pizza Dough Mix
1½ cups very warm water
2 tablespoons oil

1 container Pizza Sauce
1 package pepperoni slices
1 package shredded mozzarella cheese

In a large bowl, combine Pizza Dough Mix, very warm water, and oil; stir until a soft dough forms. Turn dough onto a lightly floured surface. Knead about 5 minutes or until dough becomes smooth and elastic, using additional flour as necessary. Cover and allow dough to rest 10 minutes. Divide dough in half and press into 2 lightly greased 12-inch pizza pans. Cover and let rise in a warm place (80 to 85 degrees) 30 minutes.

Preheat oven to 425 degrees. Bake crusts 10 minutes. Spread 1¼ cups Pizza Sauce over each partially baked crust. Place pepperoni slices on each pizza. Sprinkle 1 cup mozzarella cheese over each pizza. Bake 10 to 12 minutes or until crust is lightly browned and cheese is melted.

Yield: two 12-inch pizzas

117

PATTERNS (continued)

BANNER

NEW BABY
GIFT BAG

(Page 89)

BLANKET

It's a girl!

It's a boy!

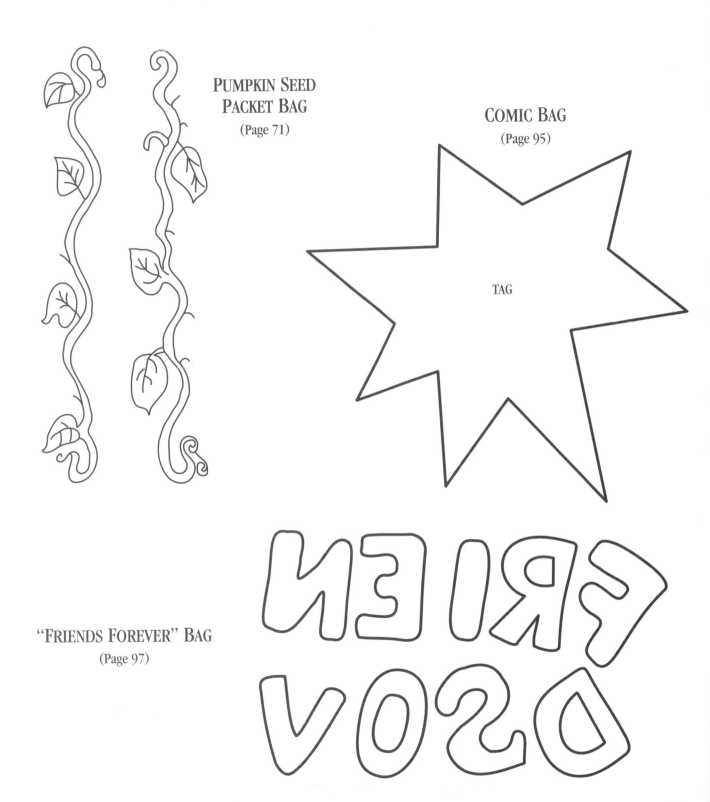

PUMPKIN SEED
PACKET BAG
(Page 71)

COMIC BAG
(Page 95)

TAG

"FRIENDS FOREVER" BAG
(Page 97)

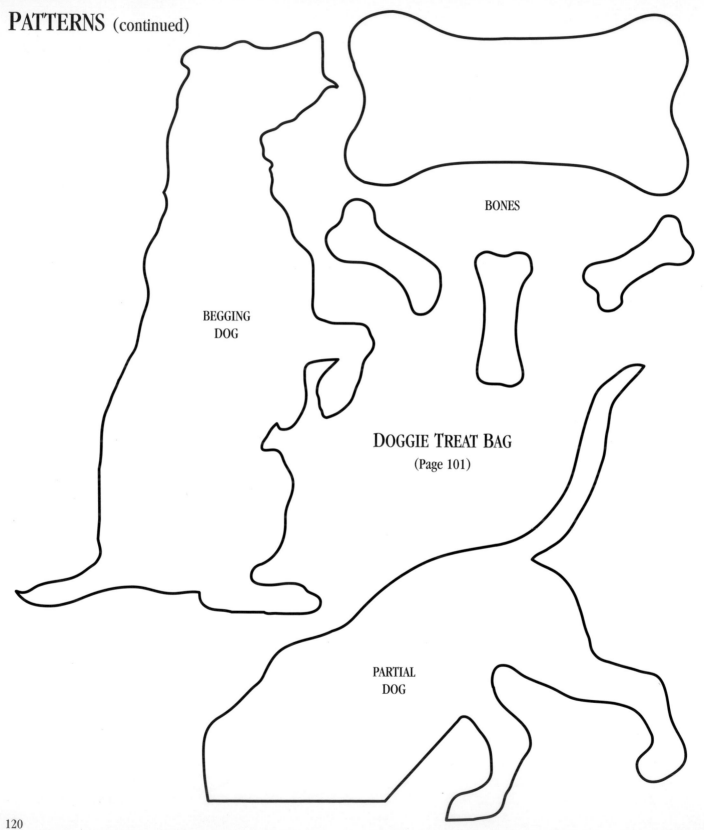

BONES

BEGGING
DOG

DOGGIE TREAT BAG

(Page 101)

PARTIAL
DOG

GENERAL INSTRUCTIONS

ABOUT THE BAGS WE USED
The following is a list of the types of purchased or ready-made bags used in this book. Measurements are for flattened bags.

Grocery bags are made of brown kraft paper and measure about 12"w x 15"h. If the printing on the front of the bag will not be covered when making a project, work on the back.
Lunch bags are made of white or brown kraft paper and measure about 6"w x 11"h.

Small brown bags are made of brown kraft paper and measure about 3½"w x 7"h.
Penny sacks are made of brown kraft paper and measure about 3"w x 5½"h.
Gift bags are the most diverse group of bags used. They come in a variety of sizes, colors, and finishes, and some have handles. We divided them into the following categories: small (about 4"w x 5½"h or smaller), medium (about 7"w x 8"h), and large (about 10"w x 13"h or larger).

ABOUT THE PAPER WE USED
For many of the projects in this book we used white and colored paper. There are a variety of papers available at copy centers or craft stores. When selecting paper, choose one that is suitable in weight for the project. We used copier paper, card and cover stock, construction paper, poster board, and Bristol board.

TRACING PATTERNS
Place tracing paper over pattern and trace pattern; cut out. For a more durable pattern, use a permanent pen to trace pattern onto acetate; cut out.

SPONGE PAINTING
Use an assembly-line approach when making several sponge painted projects. Place flattened bags on a protected work surface. Practice sponge painting technique on scrap paper until desired look is achieved. Paint all bags with first color before changing to next color. Use a clean sponge piece or shape for each additional color.

ALL-OVER SPONGE PAINTING: Dip a dampened sponge piece into paint; remove excess paint on a paper towel. Use a light stamping motion to paint item; allow to dry.

PAINTING WITH SPONGE SHAPES: Dip dampened sponge shape into paint; remove excess paint on a paper towel. Lightly press sponge shape onto project, then carefully lift sponge. Reapplying paint as necessary, repeat. To reverse a design, turn sponge shape over.

Continued on page 122

GENERAL INSTRUCTIONS (continued)

STENCILING

1. (*Note:* These instructions are written for multicolor stencils. For single-color stencils, make 1 stencil for entire design.) For first stencil, cut a piece of acetate 1" larger than entire pattern. Center acetate over pattern and use permanent pen to trace outlines of all areas of first color in stencil cutting key. For placement guidelines, outline remaining colored areas using dashed lines. Using a new piece of acetate for each additional color in stencil cutting key, repeat for remaining stencils.

2. Place each acetate piece on cutting mat and use craft knife to cut out stencil along solid lines, making sure edges are smooth.

3. Hold or tape first stencil in place. Use a clean, dry stencil brush or sponge piece. Dip brush or sponge piece in paint; remove excess paint on a paper towel. Brush or sponge piece should be almost dry to produce good results. Beginning at edge of cutout area, apply paint in a stamping motion over stencil. If desired, highlight or shade design by stamping a lighter or darker shade of paint in cutout area. Repeat until all areas of first stencil have been painted. Carefully remove stencil and allow paint to dry.

4. Using stencils in order indicated in color key and matching guidelines on stencils to previously stenciled areas, repeat Step 3 for remaining stencils.

5. To stencil a design in reverse, clean stencil and turn stencil over before using.

MAKING APPLIQUÉS

1. (*Note*: Follow all steps for each appliqué. When tracing patterns for more than 1 appliqué, leave at least 1" between shapes on web. To make a reverse appliqué, trace pattern onto tracing paper, turn traced pattern over, and follow all steps using traced pattern.) Trace appliqué pattern onto paper side of web. Cutting about ¹⁄₂" outside drawn lines, cut out web shape.

2. Follow manufacturer's instructions to fuse web shape to wrong side of fabric. Cut out shape along drawn lines.

MAKING A SEWN FABRIC BAG

1. To determine width of fabric needed, add ¹⁄₂" to desired finished width of bag. To determine length of fabric needed, double desired finished height of bag and add 1¹⁄₂". Cut a piece of fabric the determined measurements.

2. With right sides together and matching short edges, fold fabric in half; finger press folded edge (bottom of bag). Using a ¹⁄₄" seam allowance, sew sides of bag together.

3. For bag with flat bottom, match each side seam to fold line at bottom of bag; sew across each corner 1" from point (Fig. 1).

Fig. 1

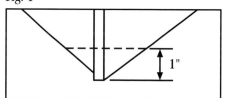

4. Press top edge of bag ¹⁄₄" to wrong side; press ¹⁄₂" to wrong side again and stitch in place.

5. Turn bag right side out.

MAKING A FUSED FABRIC BAG

1. To determine width of fabric needed, add 1" to desired finished width of bag. To determine length of fabric needed, double desired finished height of bag and add 1". Cut a piece of fabric the determined measurements.

2. (*Note:* We used ¹⁄₂" web tape for all fusing steps.) Matching right sides and short edges, press fabric piece in half (fold is bottom of bag). Unfold fabric and follow manufacturer's instructions to fuse web tape along each long edge on right side of fabric piece. Remove paper backing. Refold fabric and fuse edges together.

3. To hem bag, fuse web tape along top edge on wrong side of bag. Press edge to wrong side along inner edge of web tape. Unfold edge and remove paper backing. Refold edge and fuse in place.

4. Turn bag right side out.

JAR LID FINISHING

1. For jar lid insert, use flat part of a jar lid (same size as jar lid used in storing food) as a pattern and cut 1 circle each from cardboard, batting, and fabric. Use craft glue to glue batting circle to cardboard circle. Center fabric circle right side up on batting; glue edges of fabric circle to batting.

2. (*Caution:* If jar has been sealed in canning, be careful not to break seal of lid while following Step 2. If seal of lid is broken, jar must be refrigerated.) Remove band from filled jar; place jar lid insert in band and replace band over lid.

MAKING A MULTI-LOOP BOW

1. For first streamer, measure desired length of streamer from 1 end of ribbon and gather ribbon between fingers (Fig. 1). For first loop, keep right side facing out and fold ribbon over to form desired size loop (Fig. 2). Repeat to form another loop same size as first loop (Fig. 3). Repeat to form desired number of loops. For remaining streamer, trim ribbon to desired length.

Fig. 1   Fig. 2   Fig. 3

2. To secure bow, hold gathered loops tightly. Wrap a length of wire around center of bow. Hold wire ends behind bow, gathering all loops forward; twist bow to tighten wire. Arrange loops as desired.
3. For bow center, wrap a length of ribbon around center of bow, covering wire and overlapping ends at back; trim excess. Hot glue to secure.
4. Trim ribbon ends as desired.

MAKING A FABRIC-BACKED TAG

Follow manufacturer's instructions to fuse web to back of paper for tag center and fabric for tag background. Cut paper to desired size. Fuse fabric to poster board. Fuse paper to fabric-covered poster board. Trim fabric-covered poster board to desired width around paper.

For an easy tag, photocopy one of these designs, color and personalize it, then cut it out and attach it to your gift bag.

to:
from:

To:

From:

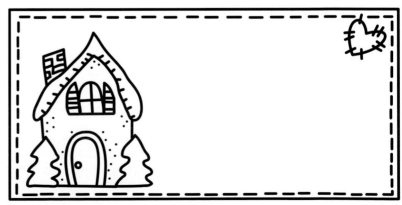

Especially for:

from: _____

KITCHEN TIPS

MEASURING INGREDIENTS

Liquid measuring cups have a rim above the measuring line to keep liquid ingredients from spilling. Nested measuring cups are used to measure dry ingredients, butter, shortening, and peanut butter. Measuring spoons are used for measuring both dry and liquid ingredients.

To measure flour or granulated sugar: Spoon ingredient into nested measuring cup and level off with a knife. Do not pack down with spoon.

To measure confectioners sugar: Sift sugar, spoon lightly into nested measuring cup, and level off with a knife.

To measure brown sugar: Pack sugar into nested measuring cup and level off with a knife. Sugar should hold its shape when removed from cup.

To measure dry ingredients equaling less than 1/4 cup: Dip measuring spoon into ingredient and level off with a knife.

To measure butter, shortening, or peanut butter: Pack ingredient firmly into nested measuring cup and level off with a knife.

To measure liquids: Use a liquid measuring cup placed on a flat surface. Pour ingredient into cup and check measuring line at eye level.

To measure honey or syrup: For a more accurate measurement, lightly spray measuring cup or spoon with cooking spray before measuring so the liquid will release easily from cup or spoon.

TESTS FOR CANDY MAKING

To determine the correct temperature of cooked candy, use a candy thermometer and the cold water test. Before each use, check the accuracy of your candy thermometer by attaching it to the side of a small saucepan of water, making sure thermometer does not touch bottom of pan. Bring water to a boil. Thermometer should register 212 degrees in boiling water. If it does not, adjust the temperature range for each candy consistency accordingly.

When using a candy thermometer, insert thermometer into candy mixture, making sure thermometer does not touch bottom of pan. Read temperature at eye level. Cook candy to desired temperature range. Working quickly, drop about 1/2 teaspoon of candy mixture into a cup of ice water. Use a fresh cup of water for each test. Use the following descriptions to determine if candy has reached the correct consistency:

Soft Ball Stage (234 to 240 degrees): Candy can be rolled into a soft ball in ice water but will flatten when held in your hand.

Firm Ball Stage (242 to 248 degrees): Candy can be rolled into a firm ball in ice water but will flatten if pressed when removed from the water.

Hard Ball Stage (250 to 268 degrees): Candy can be rolled into a hard ball in ice water and will remain hard when removed from the water.

Soft Crack Stage (270 to 290 degrees): Candy will form hard threads in ice water but will soften when removed from the water.

Hard Crack Stage (300 to 310 degrees): Candy will form brittle threads in ice water and will remain brittle when removed from the water.

SHREDDING CHEESE

To shred cheese easily, place wrapped cheese in freezer 10 to 20 minutes before shredding.

TOASTING NUTS

To toast nuts, spread nuts on an ungreased baking sheet. Stirring occasionally, bake in a 350-degree oven 8 to 10 minutes or until nuts are slightly darker in color.

PREPARING CITRUS FRUIT ZEST

To remove the zest (colored outer portion of peel) from citrus fruits, use a fine grater or fruit zester, being careful not to grate white portion of peel, which is bitter.

MELTING CHOCOLATE

To melt chocolate, place chopped or shaved chocolate in the top of a double boiler over hot, not boiling, water. Stir occasionally until chocolate melts. Remove from heat and use as desired. If necessary, chocolate may be returned to heat to remelt.

SOFTENING BUTTER OR MARGARINE

To soften 1 stick of butter, remove wrapper and place butter on a microwave-safe plate. Microwave on medium-low power (30%) 20 to 30 seconds.

SOFTENING CREAM CHEESE

To soften cream cheese, remove wrapper and place cream cheese on a microwave-safe plate. Microwave on medium power (50%) 1 to 1 1/2 minutes for an 8-ounce package or 30 to 45 seconds for a 3-ounce package.

TESTING JELLY

To determine the correct consistency of jelly made without pectin, dip a clean, dry metal spoon into the boiling jelly. Turn spoon to let jelly run from side of spoon. The jelly is ready when two drops of syrup run together to drop from the spoon in one drop or "sheet."

EQUIVALENT MEASUREMENTS

1 tablespoon	=	3 teaspoons
1/8 cup (1 fluid ounce)	=	2 tablespoons
1/4 cup (2 fluid ounces)	=	4 tablespoons
1/3 cup	=	5 1/3 tablespoons
1/2 cup (4 fluid ounces)	=	8 tablespoons
3/4 cup (6 fluid ounces)	=	12 tablespoons
1 cup (8 fluid ounces)	=	16 tablespoons or 1/2 pint
2 cups (16 fluid ounces)	=	1 pint
1 quart (32 fluid ounces)	=	2 pints
1/2 gallon (64 fluid ounces)	=	2 quarts
1 gallon (128 fluid ounces)	=	4 quarts

HELPFUL FOOD EQUIVALENTS

1/2 cup butter	=	1 stick butter
1 square baking chocolate	=	1 ounce chocolate
1 cup chocolate chips	=	6 ounces chocolate chips
2 1/4 cups packed brown sugar	=	1 pound brown sugar
3 1/2 cups unsifted confectioners sugar	=	1 pound confectioners sugar
2 cups granulated sugar	=	1 pound granulated sugar
4 cups all-purpose flour	=	1 pound all-purpose flour
1 cup shredded cheese	=	4 ounces cheese
3 cups sliced carrots	=	1 pound carrots
1/2 cup chopped celery	=	1 rib celery
1/2 cup chopped onion	=	1 medium onion
1 cup chopped green pepper	=	1 large green pepper

RECIPE INDEX

CREDITS

To Magna IV Color Imaging of Little Rock, Arkansas, we say *thank you* for the superb color reproduction and excellent pre-press preparation.

We want to especially thank photographers Larry Pennington, Mark Mathews, and Ken West of Peerless Photography, Little Rock, Arkansas, for their time, patience, and excellent work.

A special word of thanks goes to Pamela Hornsby, who contributed the recipe for the *Whipping Cream Pound Cake* on page 29.